GW00691717

Hildebrand's Travel Guide
SOUTH AFRICA

KARTO+GRAFIK VERLAGSGESELLSCHAFT MBH

Cover
Dance of the Miners
in Johannesburg

Hildebrand's Travel Guide

Publisher
K+G Verlagsgesellschaft mbH
Schönberger Weg 15
6000 Frankfurt/Main 90
West Germany

Authors
Essays: Peter Gerisch
Facts: Clausjürgen Eicke,
Hella Tarara (TAR)

Photo Credits
CJ. Eicke, Bob Martin, Eikmeier,
Hagen, Fischer, M. Goldbach, F. Swoboda,
SATOURS

Illustrations
Eckart Müller, Peter Rank, Manfred Rup

Maps
K+G, Karto+Grafik Verlagsgesellschaft mbH

Translation
Brian Mead F.I.L.

Lithography
HDR Repro, 6050 Offenbach

Type Setting
LibroSatz, 6239 Kriftel

Printed by
Klambt-Druck, 6720 Speyer

Hildebrand's Travel Guide

Part I
Impressions in pictures

Part II
Impressions in words (essays)

Part III
Information (yellow pages)

Part IV
Useful Information

Hildebrand's Travel Map

Part V
Travel Map

All rights reserved
© K+G KARTO+GRAFIK
Verlagsgesellschaft mbH
6000 Frankfurt/Main 90
1. Edition 1984
Printed in West Germany

Captions

1. The charm of daybreak in the Hluhluwe Game Reserve in the Acacia savannah: dew glistening on the grass and trees, peaceful tranquility broken only by the sounds of the game.

2. In the east the Great Escarpment drops sharply from the plateau of the "High Veld" down the lower region leading to the coast. Rivers and streams force their way downwards carving countless waterfalls – like the Matenga Falls in Swaziland shown here.

3. Many strange natural scenes are to be found in South Africa's interior – especially in the mountain areas, for the South African subcontinent is geologically one of the oldest regions in the world, with rocks up to 3 milliard years old.

4. In spring the Great Karoo – the most arid part of the Veld in the south of South Africa's highlands – blossoms into a sea of flowers and shrubs.

5. Hundreds of miles of magnificent beaches that slope shallowly into the Indian Ocean stretch along the coast of Natal. The city of Durban is foremost amongst the many bathing resorts along this coast – and not least on account of its lively "Golden Mile".

6. Beautiful beaches can be discovered between the promontories and cliffs along the ever-changing and partially segmented shore of the Cape.

7.–10. South African contrasts: here modern sober city thoroughfares like Eloff Street in Johannesburg (7) or Smith Street in Durban (8) there the colourful villages of the Ndebele tribe near Pretoria (9) or the homely Dutch architecture of Groot Constantia (10).

11./12. Sport in South Africa is a subject of great interest to young and old: whether it be their favourite game of rugby as here in Stellenbosch (11) or a mental contest of chess on a Sunday afternoon in Johannesburg's Joubert Park (12).

13.–17. Unlike the peoples of west Africa the tribes of South Africa are not pronouncedly black, but rather varying shades of dark brown. For example: Zulu (13), Herero (14), Bushman (15), Swazi (16), Tswana (17).

18. Once a mighty and proud tribe of skilled hunters, the Bushman today eke out a lowly existence – uprooted in their own land, like this Bushman family in the Kalahari.

19. Noah's ark in southern Africa: nowhere else in the Black Continent are so many species of wild animals to be found. The Kruger National Park alone shelters more than 120 types of mammals, including 19 breeds of antelope – like the kudu pictured here on the left.

20. The conservation of wildlife goes back over 300 years in South Africa. 10 national parks, several dozen provincial parks and hundreds of municipal and private game reserves give wild animals a chance to survive – including such rare species as the bontebok (photo bottom right).

21. South Africa is the home of 9,000 species of birds, from the tall white heron to the fluffy colourful lilac-breasted roller and the honeysucker (or sunbird) (centre and bottom right).

22. 16,000 to 18,000 varieties of flowers grow in South Africa – 10 times as many as in Europe. In this floral kingdom the "ruling family" is the protea and can be seen in many splendid forms (four examples are shown on the opposite page in the middle and lower rows).

23. Millions of years of erosion have turned the Fish River Canyon in southern Namibia into one of Africa's greatest natural wonders – a twisting gorge one hundred miles long and 550 m (1800 ft) deep in parts.

24. Stone Age art. There are more prehistoric "art galleries" in South Africa and Namibia than anywhere else on earth. Cave paintings and engravings vividly depict life thousands of years ago.

25. Countenance of the Namib Desert; sun-dried tufts of grass across endless stretches of sand with a background of blue, shimmering mountains.

26. "Mosi oa tunya" – the smoke that thunders: Victoria Falls on the Zambesi at the spot where Zimbabwe joins Zambia. Doubtless the most spectacular natural showpiece in Africa.

The Mother City and her fair Cape

It must have been wonderful to arrive in South Africa from Europe in the days when the steamer anchored in Cape Town harbour. The mighty Table Mountain with its two foothills, Lion's Head and Signal Hill (best seen on land from Blouberg beach on the far side of Table Bay), rose majestically out of the sea, and as the shore grew nearer the passengers could well imagine why Sir Francis Drake in 1580 had called the Cape of Good Hope (which, of course, cannot be seen from Table Bay) "the fairest cape we saw in the whole circumference of the earth".

Today's tourist arrive in Cape Town mainly by plane, car or with the "Blue Train" – the latter arriving equally impressively at the central station at the foot of Table Mountain. When they step out they are standing in the middle of Adderley Street, Cape Town's main road, that is the continuation of Heerengracht, leading to the port; these two street names reflect the city's mixed Dutch-British past. Where they meet there is a statue of Jan van Riebeeck and his wife, Maria – symbolically carved half by a mason in London and half by a Dutchman in Den Haag.

In 1488 the Portuguese mariner Bartholomaus Diaz landed in a bay on the peninsula which he mistook to be Table Bay and which has since been called False Bay. He was soon followed by his compatriot Vasco da Gama, who gave the name "Cabo da Boa Esperanca", but it was the Dutchman Jan van Riebeeck who established a supply post for the Dutch East India Company in 1652 and laid the foundations for the present day Cape Town. A look at the atlas shows that Cape Town is roughly halfway between the Netherlands and what is now called Indonesia.

Out of the "vegetable garden", as some South Africans still affectionately call that first settlement (and which above all supplied fresh drinking water) grew South Africa's "Mother city" – its nickname today. Many enthusiasts consider it one of the most beautifully located cities in the whole world and compare it to Rio de Janeiro.

Comparisons leave a lot to be desired, so let us look at the facts. Cape Town's irrefutable charm lies in the harmonious blend of past and present. Between elegant old Cape Dutch houses (that will be described in a separate chapter) modern high-rise office blocks on a par with Johannesburg have sprung up and beneath them lie vast underground shopping precincts. Naturally, an important element of the city's charm is its position at the foot of Table Mountain whose plateau rises abruptly from sea level to 3,500 feet and which can be reached in a dizzy ascent in a cable-car or in a three hour walk. The jaunt in the cable-car lasts only five minutes, but still causes a few wobbly knees. However, the view from the top makes it well worth it.

A further part of Cape Town's charm is its dual hinterland: the peninsula in the south and the varied countryside of western Cape Province on its north, east and southeast flanks with the mountain ranges of Franschhoek, Wemmershoek, Dutoits, Slanghoek, Hottentots Holland and the old townships of Stellenbosch, Wellington, Worcester, Somerset West, Franschhoek, Caledon and others.

For those who prefer to get their first impressions of a place from high up, Signal Hill makes a good starting point as an alternative to taking the cableway up to Table Mountain. Signal Hill can be reached by car, and from a height of 1,200 feet affords a magnificent view of the city by day or night. Don't let the canon blast worry you; it is only a remote controlled signal from the South African Astronomical Observatory that it is midday, and it reminds one that arriving ships were formerly announced in this manner – thus giving the hill its name. Nor should one be worried at night by the courting couples for whom Signal Hill is a traditional trysting place.

From there you can see the Castle of Good Hope, built in 1666 and the oldest building in South Africa (proving how young a country it is). Once the residence of the Cape's first Governor it now serves as a garrison for the army, housing a War Museum, a Maritime Museum, the lovely William Fehr collection of antique furniture and porcelain, old masters and glassware.

This collection gives an idea of the elegance of bygone days in the Cape.

In South Africa regard for national heritage and possessions is shown by declaring them historical monuments. Both Table Mountain and the cobble-stoned Greenmark Square – where people took a leisurely evening stroll during the 17th and 18th centuries – have been bestowed this honour. Near this square, on the far side of Adderley Street, is the Flower Market that resembles a sea of blossom on weekday mornings.

At the other end Adderley Street runs into Government Avenue whose name is belied by the fine old oaks and buildings that line its pathway: the Anglican cathedral of St. George's, the South African Public Library, the Houses of Parliament, the Cultural History Museum in the building that was formerly the Higher Court, and the Company's Garden – a part of van Riebeeck's original vegetable gardens. The Tuynhuis (Garden House) opposite dates from 1751 and is the residence of the Head of State when parliament sits. The Grand Parade next to the castle is a reminder of Dutch colonial times when it was used for military parades. It is a sign of the times that nowadays it is used as a second-hand market on Wednesdays and Saturdays.

There is a lot to see in Cape Town: for example, the Malay Quarter – the traditional area of the Cape Malays, descendants of slaves or political refugees from the Far East in the 17th century. Together with the whites, blacks and Indians they make up the multi-racial state with all its resultant problems.

Then there is the Peninsula, 30 miles long and 10 miles across at its widest point, terminating in Cape Point, that, you may be disappointed to discover, is not – as often supposed – the southern-most point of the African Continent. This privilege falls to Cape Agulhas further to the south-east. However, Cape Point can claim to be the spot where the Atlantic joins the Indian Ocean.

The traditional day trip along the peninsula is down the 90 mile long Marine Drive from Cape Town along the west coast through the suburbs of Green Point, Clifton Bay and Camps Bay and along the Twelve Apostles rock formation as far as the fishing village of Hout Bay, so called because the Dutch East India Company hewed the wood for its ships' masts here.

The journey along Chapman's Peak Drive is breathtaking; 500 feet below on the right-hand side the ocean crashes against the rocks, on the left Chapman's Peak towers 1,000 feet above your head. After driving through the two resorts Kommetjie and Witsands, you pass through the nature reserve on the southern tip of the peninsula and finally arrive at Cape Point. From the car park it can cost some effort to reach the light house if you fail to get a seat on the bus, "The Flying Dutchman". In any case, everybody has to cover the last 40 yards on foot, but the sight of the two oceans meeting from 700 feet up is well worth the effort.

The return journey takes you back through the Cape of Good Hope Nature Reserve, through Smitswinkel and past False Bay up the east side of the peninsula to Simonstown, the headquarters of the South African Navy. Further on comes Fish Hoek, the picturesque fishing port in Kalk Bay, and St. James, where one can view the house in which Cecil Rhodes died in 1902. Muizenberg with its long stretch of beach and promenade is one of the peninsula's favourite seaside resorts and – as it is sheltered from the Atlantic breakers – one of the safest.

From here one can either take the inland motorway straight back to Cape Town or do like most other day-trippers and visit Groot Constantia, considered one of the finest examples of Cape Dutch architecture (this will be dealt with in a later chapter). The residential mansion and its adjacent buildings make up a majestic property that was erected in 1685 for Governor Simon van Stel. It is now a museum with a wine exhibition in the cellar.

If there is time enough, and provided you are not exhausted from the day's new experiences, you could still drop in on the National Botanical Gardens in Kirstenbosch (see next page) on the way back. The Cape is not only one of the most charming in the world, but also one of the most strenuous. (See the special map on page 128.)

The Cape of Good Blossom

On my first visit to South Africa I was fully prepared for the wild animals, for the gold mines, the Zulu kraals and the mile-long beaches, but not for the masses of wild flowers. The greater was the excitement of my first confrontation with the flora on the Cape of Good Hope. It was in spring, and behind Table Mountain nature had exploded in infinite blossom.

Nowhere in the world are there so many types of wild plants in such a small area – less than 200 square miles – as in the Cape. They shoot out of the ground with more power than words can describe, bearing witness to the latent strength that languishes in this young land. Both Charles Darwin (1809–1882) and the Swedish botanist Carl von Linné (1707–1778) before him were equally impressed.

Certain climatic factors determine the specific nature of flora on the Cape. In the dry season light mists mollify the summer heat around Table Mountain, so that at 4,500 feet plants blossom and flourish like the delicate Blue Drip Disa orchid that grows in the humid moss here between the rock fissures and nowhere else on earth. In winter north-westerlies bring rain to the south and south-easterly slopes of the Table Mountain plateau, creating an extraordinary accumulation of varieties, of which the Erica, or Cape heather, with over a 100 species is the biggest. Over and above that there are at least 17 more genera with 20 or more inter-related varieties, including oxalis, crassula, pelargonie, helichrysum, orchids and gladiolli.

In comparison, the British Isles are 500 times larger, yet list only 2 genera with more than 20 varieties.

The most prominent among the Cape flora is the Protea, South Africa's national flower. When establishing his nomenclature Linné gave this flower the name Proteus, a Greek god who was a master of transformation, and the flower does the name credit, ranging from tall plants to ground-creepers; some sport strikingly spiral-shaped blossoms, others small, drooping or even hidden ones; some look like roses, others like thistles; some are shaped like pencils, while others resemble Catherine-wheels or pin cushions. The hues are pallid and shiny – red, white, pink, apricot, silver, yellow or green.

The best place to see the Cape flora in concentrated form is in the Kirstenbosch National Botanical Gardens on the east slopes of Table Mountain that are exclusively given over to the cultivation of indigenous flowers and plants, and a meeting place for enthusiasts and biologists from all over the world.

At the end of my first visit to South Africa some newly-aquired friends – it is a good place for making friends quickly – presented me with a bouquet of flowers from the Cape of Good Hope. It stood five feet high and had to be stowed in the aircraft luggage hold.

Cape Town to Port Elizabeth via the Garden Route

South Africa's most famous highway is rather like women's fashions – longer or shorter according to taste. The beginning and end of the Garden Route vary according to the description. What is sure is that it is the National Road N2 that joins Cape Town to Port Elizabeth, tempting protagonists of the maxi-style to take these two cities as start and finish and thus arriving at 467 miles. Those preferring the mini only recognize the 130 mile section between Mossel Bay in the west and the estuary of Storms River into the Indian Ocean in the east, this being undoubtedly the prettiest and most varied stretch of countryside of the whole route.

Let us compromise and add the 110 miles from Swellendam to Mossel Bay in the west and the 60 miles from Storms River to Jeffrey's Bay in the east.

Swellendam, picturesquely situated at the foot of the Langeberg mountains 140 miles from Cape Town, was founded in 1747 and with Tulbagh is the third oldest town in the republic. In its oak-lined street you will still discover Cape Dutch buildings, amongst them Old Drostdy, once the district Commissioner's. Not far away on the banks of the river Bree there is the Bontebok National Park established primarily to preserve this 3 ft tall antelope, threatened with extinction.

Passing through Heidelberg, Riversdale with the interesting Julius Gordon Africana Museum and its collection of South African civilization, and Albertina the N2 leaves its inland course and joins the coast at Mossel Bay, becoming the Garden Route by any definition. It was here that Bartholomaus Diaz first set foot on South African soil in 1488 even before landing at the Cape Peninsula.

The biggest, and at the same time, the most original object of interest at Mossel Bay is the Post Office tree; a milkwood tree that has been used as a post office since 1500, when a sailor on route to the East Indies left a message hanging there in his boot. It was found a year later by other sailors and became a custom that is still followed today. Letters can be posted in a boot-shaped letter-box and are cancelled with a special stamp. Under the tree is a fresh-water spring discovered by Diaz and still flowing. Both the spring and the tree have been declared historical monuments – how could it be otherwise in South Africa.

60 miles north of Mossel Bay over the Robinson Pass in the Outeniqua Mountains lies Oudtshoorn in the Little Karoo region. This little town is counted as part of the Garden Route because of its tourist attractions which include the ostrich farms (see special chapter) and the Cango caves. The section that is open to the public consists of eight caves and passages spread over five miles

and full of spectacular stalagmites and stalactites. The biggest grotto has such fine acoustics that concerts are held there.

Taking the road from Oudtshoorn over the Outeniqua Pass back towards the Indian Ocean, one arrives at George the next stop on the Garden Route. After visiting this area in 1780 the French ornithologist, Francois Levaillant (1753–1824), raved in his book – Journey to Africa's interior by way of The Cap of Good Hope 1780–1785 – "Here were we privileged to see the most beautiful land in the universe. In the distance we could view the mountains mantled in proud forests, concealing the horizon… beneath us lay the extensive valley, decorated with well-formed hills sloping in waves down to the sea". The citizens of George believe they inhabit the "world's prettiest and smallest village" – two quotes that speak for themselves.

Even so, the next town with the misleading name of The Wilderness is no less beautiful. A five mile long beach with almost snow-white sand leads up to the mouth of the river Touw. From the estuary to Swartvlei Lagoon at Sedgefield in the east lie The Lakes – an almost uninterrupted expanse of water much loved by South African holiday-makers.

Knysna, situated on the Knysna Heads lagoon in the shelter of the rocks, has a romantic past, being founded by George IV, then Prince of Wales, during a visit to South Africa in 1797, and Hanna Lighfoot, the Quaker. A significant timber industry was built up and the local port used for shipping out. The railway put an end to this in 1928 and all that remains are joineries making furniture out of the beautiful stinkwood and yellowwood, felled in the 15 separate woods that make up the Knysna Forest and cover an area of 200,000 acres.

The Garden Route now dips into these forests which are the home of the Knysna elephants. Although these are amongst the biggest in the world there is no reason to worry for they are extremely shy and hide away in South Africa's extensive forest-land.

Over the Keurbooms River and through the pretty resort of Nature's Valley – a fitting name for a community that is also a nature reserve – and on up to the Groot River Pass from where there is a breath-taking view of the Groot River estuary and Nature's Valley. As though this were not enough, five miles beyond this pass another mountain road begins winding its way in a series of hairpin bends through the jungle up to the equally spectacular Bloukrans Pass.

The Route now runs between two national parks. On the right the 900 yard wide Tsitsikamma Coastal National Park runs parallel to the coastline for the 50 miles from the Groot River estuary at Nature's Valley to a second Groot River west of Humansdorp. This park is intended to preserve the marine life along this rugged rocky shore. On the left, north of the National Road, lies the Tsitsikamma Forest National Park replete with yellowwood trees some estimated to be 850 years old. The most prominent is simply called The Big Tree and stands 300 yards from the road from where it can be reached by a footpath.

And now comes the pride of South Africa's bridges, the Paul Sauer Bridge that elegantly spans the Storms River in a 630 foot long, 455 foot high bow. This is the end of the main part of the Garden Route. In the nearby National Parks Board restaurant is an exhibition of photos showing the bridge during construction and a small but interesting museum.

The countryside now becomes less interesting for the eye but more so for the palate since Humansdorp, 54 miles east of the Paul Sauer Bridge, lies in the heart of sheep and farming country. Now it is less than 9 miles to Jeffreys Bay, an El Dorado for surf-riders on the wide St. Francis Bay. 25 miles further on, in the public library at Port Elizabeth, there is a collection of mussels, mostly found on the shore of St. Francis Bay – a pretty end to a Route that – with its ever-changing coastline, mountains, forests, lakes and mountain passes – is more than just a nice garden.

There is also a collection of more than 1,000 types of mussels in Mossel Bay and if you go there between May and September you can enjoy fresh oysters, considered the best on the entire Garden Route.

The elegant Cape Dutch Gable

In December 1967 Professor Christiaan Barnard made the hospital in Cape Town with the name Groote Schuur world famous, when he performed the first heart transplant in history. The Dutch name means "Great Barn" and is obviously not intended to be a comment on the hospital rather having been named after the official Cape Town residence of the South African Prime Minister nearby. This, in turn, has been so called because the granaries belonging to the Dutch East India Company once stood on this spot.

It is not only names like this that today serve as a reminder that the Dutch once settled in the southern tip of Africa, but above all the Cape Dutch architecture that reached its peak in the 18th century and is notable for its elegance and the magnificence of its gables.

The first settlers' houses were simply square with a gable at each end as in the mother country. But as they prospered the settlers craved for a status symbol on their homes, and this led to the idea of constructing decorative gables in the middle of the long side of the houses. These gables were also rather practical, letting more light into the loft, keeping the rain away from the front door and providing better protection if the thatched roof caught fire.

Early middle-gables were triangular, gradually adopting the characterically whirly decorations during the course of the 18th century. Under the influence of baroque art in Europe they became – particularly amongst the rich landowners – more luxuriously ornamented with spirals and embossings, sometimes extending over the entire frontage.

The charm of Cape Dutch architecture, especially in the vine-country around Cape Town, is the way it blends with the surrounding countryside. The lime-washed houses stand up against the green vineyards and the blue hue of the distant mountains. The Cape Province sun reflects gently off the uneven surface, forming soft shadows around the ornamentation and embracing every pattern in a wonderful luminous light.

A great number of Cape Dutch houses in Cape Town and the vicinity have been turned into historical monuments and are open to the public. In the town itself are: The Old Supreme Court, now a culture museum; the adjacent Koopmans de Wet House; the Martin Melck House; The Old Town House, currently an art gallery, and the house with the charming name of Rust-en-Vreugd (Peace and Joy) that houses the William Fehr collection of historical paintings and etchings.

The most famous example of Cape Dutch architecture in the vicinity is Groot Constantia. Once the residence of the Dutch governor Simon von der Stel until his death in

1712, Groot Constantia is included on every coach excursion. In addition, there is Alphen, now a hotel, and Kronendal, currently used as a restaurant and antique shop. In Stellenbosch – South Africa's second oldest city after Cape Town – two buildings merit a mention, Burger House and Libertas Parva. In Paarl there stands the Oude Pastorie – a Cape Dutch name that probably does not require translation.

A Treat for Train Spotters

Here is an itinerary that for train enthusiasts is the equivalent of a menu in a five star restaurant for gourmets: "The train is pulled in series by steam engines of the 25 NC, 15 CA, 24 and 15 F classes. Stops are made during the journey to enable photos of the most attractive parts of the route to be taken". This and similar texts attract train enthusiasts from all over the world to take part in Steam Safaris lasting several days that are organised throughout the year by the South African Railways.

These enthusiasts were possibly amongst the few people who were glad about the oil crisis in 1974 because it halted the South African railways' intensive programme of electrification and slowed down the introduction of diesel-driven engines as there are large coal reserves in the country. So today there are still 1,600 steam engines in service, making South Africa a Mecca for train-lovers. They are mainly in service on local routes, but also on main lines like the one that leads through the Great Karoo from Kimberley to De Aar. Along this stretch lies the tiny station of Kraankuil. Every day 50 engines puff past, making it a very special location for train spotters.

Naturally, there are also excellent narrow gauge railways in South Africa, the best example being the "Apple Express". From Port Elizabeth on the Indian Ocean across the orchard country of Langkloof – where predominantly apples are grown – to Avontuur lie 178 miles of 24″ gauge railway track – the longest of its type in the world. The fruit-laden wagons are usually drawn

by diesels nowadays, but on most Saturdays between the beginning of May and the end of January – outside the apple season – the South African Railways organise special trips with steam engines and old time wagons dating from the start of the century. The journey from Port Elizabeth to Loerie and back totals only 90 miles, but takes the whole day.

A special piece of railway fascination can be seen in Fauresmith in the Orange Free State – the trains drive right through the centre of the town.

If any train enthusiast would like to correspond with a counterpart in South Africa he should contact: The Secretary, Railway Society of Southern Africa, P.O. Box 9775, Johannesburg 2000, Republic of South Africa.

In a very appropriate place, namely the Johannesburg Central Station, there is the South African Railway Museum with an exhibition of historically interesting railway objects. Anyone who would like to see another exciting exhibition of this nature should go to Bulawayo in neighbouring Zimbabwe.

Oudtshoorn – Stronghold of the Ostrich

So that's what it feels like to sit on an ostrich. Quite nice, provided the bird doesn't start running, for they can get up to 40 mph. But here at Highgate Farm near the little town of Oudtshoorn in the west of Cape Province the bird stands in a rump stall, a kind of wooden straightjacket, and cannot get away. One after another the visitors from a group touring the farm climb on its back for the obligatory snapshot. Even Professor Christiaan Barnard allowed himself to be photographed in this position. For the widely-travelled tourist who has had his picture taken on the back of a camel in Egypt, on a mule or donkey on a Mediterranean island, on an elephant in In-

dia or even on a giant turtle in the Seychelles, South Africa is probably the only place on earth he can complete his collection with an ostrich photo.

In 1850 Alec Hooper, a bank clerk from Highgate in London, arrived with his family in the little town of Oudtshoorn in the middle of the Little Karoo where ostriches had just started being bred for their feathers, the area being climatically ideal. When the land of the company Hooper worked for was divided up 28 years later, he bought a section, named it after his birth-place and began breeding his own ostriches, just at a time when ostrich feathers were in great demand in Europa and

America for ladies' accessories. So a blooming industry developed in Oudtshoorn with as many legends and stories woven around it as in the gold and diamond centres. At the turn of the century there are said to have been more millionaires in Oudtshoorn – called Feather Barons – than in Johannesburg. Their stately homes were referred to as Ostrich Palaces. One good example is the Welgeluk Residence on Safari Farm near Oudtshoorn.

However, the whims of fashion put an abrupt end to ostrich breeding soon after the First World War, and from then on ostrich feathers were only needed for film and theatre costumes and such mundane things as dusters, forcing many farmers to look for other products. Naturally, some held on for Oudtshoorn is the only place on earth where ostriches are commercially reared and 99 per cent of the world's tame ostriches come from this area.

Today there are still 350 ostrich breeders with a total of some 90,000 birds, all descendants of the herds that used to roam wild in the region. Thanks to improved breeding methods and nutrition the quality of the feathers has risen significantly with the result that at the present time a kilo of feathers costs between £150 and £275, depending on the quality – not a bad price when one considers that each ostrich produces one kilo every nine months. 85 per cent of the feathers are exported, the rest being made into products like the duster already mentioned locally. Incidentally, plucking is quite painless for the ostrich; the larger feathers are cut and the smaller ones fall out naturally.

The Hoopers stayed true to the ostrich, too; the fifth generation still resides on the 1,500 acres of Highgate Farm and has carried the business a stage further. Shortly before the Second World War the owner

was asked to show his estate to a group of overseas visitors. This soon became known and more and more viewers came. The Hoopers then decided to turn their grounds into a show-place that now hosts 50,000 interested guests annually. No other family in South Africa has done as much to make the ostrich known as the Hoopers.

At Highgate – as at the second show farm around Oudtshoorn, the Safari Farm with its Ostrich Palace – every day throughout the year from early morning to late afternoon two-hour tours take place. Multi-lingual guides explain all the aspects of this unusual industry to the visitors, who are shown the enclosures where herds of 100 or 150 birds of about the same age are grouped together. Those with high quality feathers are put to stud. A male and a female are fenced in an area measuring about two and a half acres, where they remain for the rest of their lives – a period of up to 40 years. An ostrich gives its best feathers when it is between three and twelve years old.

About 14 days after mating the first egg is laid, followed by another every two days until between 12 and 15 have been laid. The eggs take 42 days to hatch, during which time both birds take turns to sit on them – the females in the daytime, the males at night. The chicks have brown speckles and blend perfectly with their background. They take two years to grow to full size. Males are able to kick savagely forwards and with their sharp toe-nails can be extremely dangerous. This is why the farmers arm themselves with a thorny branch before entering the enclosures and hatching areas.

In 1963, as the local Rotary Club was looking for special attractions for a charity show, the Hoopers came up with an idea that has since become a firm part of the tour. Workers on the farm don jockey colours and have amusing but fast ostrich races. Another part of the visitors' programme is an exhibition of objects the birds have swallowed. It is surprising the things that can pass down an ostrich's neck – even hair curlers.

On both farms there are big souvenir shops that offer, amongst other things, articles made out of ostrich leather: handbags, brief cases, wallets, spectacle cases, purses, shoes, jackets and coats. These articles can also be purchased in leather and clothes shops in town. Even the eggs are depleted of their contents, steam-cleaned inside and out, painted with the traditional symbols of the native tribes, and offered as rather voluminous souvenirs. In their natural state these eggs weigh between two and three pounds and taste delicious, especially as omelets – one egg providing up to 20.

Ostrich meat can be roasted or eaten raw, in which case it is salted and dried and then called biltong. This is served as a farewell snack on both show farms and is definitely an acquired taste, though those born and bred in Oudtshoorn eat it the way other people eat peanuts.

Private Game Reserves – the Animal Kingdom on Foot.

The excitement is high. Eight of us treading through the middle of the wild animal domain in the eastern Transvaal bush, keeping an eye open for elephants, lions, leopards, rhinoceroses, and thankfully less dangerous creatures like the ubiquitous impala. Luckily, we are led by an experienced game-keeper and his assistant, who, to be on the safe side, is armed.

What – with only a few exceptions – is strictly forbidden in South African public game reserves, is the main attraction in the private ones. And if the safari cannot be undertaken on foot, then there is always the station wagon. The advantage being that the tourists don't have to jostle at the windows to take photos, so that I can keep filming the menacing approach of the mother elephant and her young until the driver moves off.

Private game reserves are relatively new in South Africa, and over a dozen have sprung up mostly along the western border of the Kruger National Park in the last few years. These belong to farmers who have gone over to wildlife conservation and offer game lodges that are quite differently equipped to the national and provincial reserves.

In the latter the policy is to provide the visitor with roof over his head, a bed, a bathroom with the bare essentials, and just enough food to keep him from starving. The game lodges are the exact opposite. Not only do they put the visitor in the intimate presence of his almost "personal" game-keeper, but also provide a high degree of comfort in the middle of the bush. The lodges usually consist of luxuriously appointed bungalows with air-conditioning and bathrooms, elegant club houses with imaginative architecture and licensed bars – very important in South Africa –, swimming pools with constantly purified water, landing fields for light aircraft that ferry guests from the large airports, and a "boma" – a bamboo stockade where first class evening meals are served around a crackling fire and under a ceiling of stars.

This luxury in the wilderness is not frowned upon by serious minded environmentalists, but regarded as an effective means of creating funds with which to promote wildlife preservation. This is proved by the fact that the private game reserves enjoy the moral support of the highly respected Wildlife Society of Southern Africa.

There is an inimitable charm in sitting on a lodge terrace in the evening and swopping stories with other guests about the day's events. Naturally, these stories revolve around the wild animals, that are just as varied as in the neighbouring Kruger National Park.

When I open the door of my bungalow the next morning, an enormous kudu antelope tries to force his way in with his corkscrew-shaped horns. Fortunately, the bungalow has a back entrance, and I slip out – right into the middle of peaceful herd of grazing zebras that had followed the kudus into the camp. What a way to start the day!

Diamond Hunting – Strictly against the Law

Shimmering green rainwater that has gathered in the huge crater prevents a view of the bottom a remarkable 2,500 feet below. Remarkable since the hole was made by human hand. The panorama from the observation platform on the edge of the Big Hole is the chief attraction at Kimberley, stronghold of the diamond industry. The most gigantic hand-made crater in the world measures 1,500 feet across, has a circumference of almost a mile and covers an area of over 40 acres. In the years from 1871 to 1914, 25 million tons of "blue earth" were extracted, from which the treasure hunters produced 15 million carats, or three tons, of diamonds.

After the Big Hole, a visit to the open-air museum gives an impression of life during the diamond-rush, that could well be compared to the days of the wild west. You can view the oldest house in town that was transported by ox-cart. Furthermore, a blacksmith's, the first Lutheran church, and, of course, a saloon. In the diamond exhibition can be seen an uncut stone of 616 carat – the largest ever mined at Kimberly, and that as late as 1974.

On the other side of the town, visitors can watch the day-to-day workings in the De Beers mine from another observation platform. A by-product of the diamond industry –

and a very essential one – are the kennels outside Kimberley, where the dogs that guard the De Beer Company property are bred and trained. Perhaps the ulterior motive in having the kennels open to the public is to frighten off potential diamond thieves!

Although it is against the law for amateurs to gather precious stones outside the mines, they are allowed to look for the semi-precious stones for which the country is also famous. The exception is emeralds, which may only be mined in commercial enterprises. Amongst the most favoured semi-precious stones that amateur mineralogists from all over the world come to search for every year are tiger's-eye, found mostly in the north of Cape Province, jasper from the same region, agate from the banks of the Vaal and the river Orange, amethyst in the Keimoes, Kakamas, Uppington and Pofadder districts in north-west Cape Province, serpentine from eastern transvaal, and amazonite also from around Pofadder.

These stones are most easily found in the slag-heaps of operating or abandoned mines. Permission to search should, therefore, be got from the company concerned, the farmer on whose land the mine ist situated, or from the local authorities. A good place to get information concerning the whereabouts of semi-precious stones is the local police station. Probably the only place on earth where you can "ask a policeman" about picking up valuable gems is South Africa.

Shopping with a Passport

When purchasing jewellery of gold or precious stones it is often worth while to carry your passport and return ticket, if possible with the flight already entered. You can then go to a VSJ jeweller who possesses a customs permit allowing him to sell gems to foreigners on presentation of the documents mentioned at 13 per cent below the list price. Further information is available from The Jewellery Council of South Africa, Kine Centre, Commissioner Street, Johannesburg – telephone 0 11– 21 56 31.

South Africa is a shopper's paradise. The biggest shopping precinct in the country is the Carlton Centre in Johannesburg that spreads out over five blocks and comprises more than 160 shops. But in the city and its immediate surroundings alone there are 20 more shopping areas.

There are bargains to be had in both men's and women's clothing. Swakara hides from the Namibian caracul sheep are regarded as the most versatile fur after mink – its colours ranging from snow-white or grey to classical black with a series of brown hues in between. For men there are safari suits, which prove very practical in the game reserves and can even be worn at home on hot summer days.

The curio shops, in which native handmade goods are sold, are a world of their own. Probably the biggest in the country is the African Art

Centre in the Guildhall Arcade next to Gardiner Street in Durban, although these shops are to be found all over the country.

In them you can buy wonderful hand-woven carpets made of caracul wool and enriched with the traditional ornaments of the various tribes. These carpets can be laid on the floor or hung on the wall at home. Then there are all sorts of ornaments carved out of the wood of the olive, tamboti or red ivory-tree – three of the most beautiful woods in Africa. There is also a wide variety of woven goods and wickerwork on offer.

Many tourists like to collect exotic music, not only as records or cassettes but also in the form of the instruments on which it is played, and these are available in most curio shops. Instruments like the mbira or the mbila, consisting of a number of small pipes that remind one of an early harpsichord and bring forth very melodious sounds. Other favourite souvenirs are bush drums in every shape and size, and pod rattles made up of hollow seed pods that are bound together and tied to the ankles and wrists of the dancers, thereby producing a rhythmic sound.

South Africa also offers excellently finished goods made of hides and ostrich leather – the latter was fully explained in the chapter dealing with a visit to an ostrich farm.

Johannesburg – a Golden Experience

No other town in the world presents such a view from the air as Johannesburg. The slag-heaps from the gold-mines – that some enthusiastically call the "new pyramids of Africa" – loom up around the city; mighty honey-coloured hills, some savagely fragmented, others with perfect geometrical shapes. This is what remains of the 1,600 million tons of rock that have been reduced to powder in the course of the past hundred years to extract 100 million Troy ounces of gold: for one ton only produces as much gold dust as the salt needed for a boiled egg.

The sight of these "pyramids" arouses in every newcomer the wish – if not already there – to visit a gold-mine. Naturally enough, day-trips out to the mines at Witwatersrand are primarily intended for businessmen and mining experts who either fly to Welkom, Klerksdorp or Orkney, or board the coach to Evander or Carletonville. Groups are quite unacceptable: individual requests listing alternative dates should be sent in writing two or three months in advance to: The Public Relations Advisor, Chamber of Mines of South Africa, P.O.Box 809, Johannesburg 2000. Telephone 0 11–8 38 82 11.

Nevertheless, since 1980 there has been an establishment open to everyone only 4 miles south of Johannesburg that has developed into one of the most frequented spots in South Africa – The Gold Mining Museum of the Chamber of Mines of South Africa.

It is on the site of the former Crown Mines that up till 1978 had produced more gold than any other mine in the world – 1,500 tons. 30,000 miners, workers, and clerks were employed here. Nowadays this museum gives visitors the chance to literally get the feel of a gold-mine. Before descending to what was once Pit 14 700 feet under ground, you are fitted out with oil-skins, boots, and, of course, a miner's helmet complete with lamp. You will be guided by an experienced miner

But the gear at ground level is fascinating, too, and the three hours that a tour lasts slip past like – if you'll excuse the expression – gold-dust through your fingers. Every half hour you can witness gold bars being poured and many spectators consider this experience the climax of their entire South African holiday. Even the out-dated process of panning off is demonstrated, and afterwards visitors can try their own luck in a stream close-by.

An historically authentic miners' village with houses maintained in their original state, a blacksmith's, and a veteran steam-engine help re-create the atmosphere from 1886, when a digger named George Harrison discovered the main gold vein at Witwatersrand, up to 1920.

The geological exhibition, showing the formation of the rich gold veins in the Transvaal and Orange Free State, is extremely interesting as well. After all that sightseeing, visitors can not only take a meal in the Crown Reef Restaurant – a replica of a miner's boarding house from 1915 –, but also purchase articles of gold at the jeweller's and that, if they are foreign tourists, duty-free.

The large arena that sits 2,500 deserves our special attention, because here every morning and afternoon during the week African tribal dances take place. But the highlight comes every Sunday at 11 am and 2 pm, when active miners perform. The Zulus, Bacas, Pondos, Xhosas, Shangaans and members of other tribes dance in their vivid traditional costumes for their own pleasure, and spectators are merely tolerated. A fury of wild yet controlled movements with a defined meaning give this spectacle its real and unmistakeable charm, making it a treat for amateur photographers, especially if equipped with a zoom lense.

Small wonder that the Sunday performances in particular are so popular, and one is well advised to reserve seats in advance. This can be done through the Marketing Department, Gold Mine Museum, P.O.-Box 809, Johannesburg 2000. Telephone 0 11–8 35 10 27, extension 14. The Marketing Department also organises group visits for English and non-English speakers, emphasizing the importance attributed to the foreign buyers of that "international currency" – the Kruger Rand.

At present 400,000 people work in the South African gold-mines – making the industry one of the biggest employers in the world. More than 250,000 work underground, some of them at depths of 10,000 feet below ground. In spite of the pit-heads being some 5,000 feet above sea level, the gold-bearing rock is extracted from much lower than the ocean bed that borders the African continent.

It is hard to believe that the history of gold in the Transvaal only goes back a hundred years. The first quartz containing gold was mined in the seventies of the last century at Eersteling near Pietersburg. The mine was closed down in 1877 because mechanical mining was costlier than the panning operations at Barberton and Pilgrim's Rest. Then in 1886 George Harrison made the sensational discovery at Witwatersrand, so called on account of the light colour of the water ("white water") that ran off the sides of the hills following the summer rains.

Johannesburg, that took root north of the mines on the main vein, was only an encampment of tents and covered wagons to start with. As geologists ascertained that under the 50 mile east-west vein were more, a modern industrial mining centre able to excavate and refine immense amounts of rock profitably developed. From this mining centre a proper city grew up that with almost two million inhabitants is the biggest mining establishment in the world and the hub of the South African gold refining industry.

The workmanship of Johannesburg's goldsmiths is of the very highest quality. How foreign visitors can buy these goods without having to pay the 13 per cent duty was explained in the chapter "Shopping with a Passport".

The most Luxurious Train in the World.

Dinner, served on snow-white table-cloths in the finest china by immaculately dressed waiters, consists of Shrimp Cocktail, Celementine Cream Soup or Fried Sole with Tartar Sauce. For the main course Veal Maréchal with asparagus in cream sauce, Roast Turkey or Joint of Lamb, both garnished with a selection of vegetables. Finally, Steam Pudding with Egg Custard or Peach Melba, cheese, coffee and biscuits.

We are not talking about an expensive cruise or a five-star hotel, but about the most luxurious train available to the general public in the world today; a paragon of self-indulgence for its own sake, the purpose of which is not simply to get passengers from one place to another as quickly as the rails will allow. We are talking about the "Blue Train" that plies between Pretoria and Cape Town via Johannesburg. Officially a part of the South African Transport Services, it is really a state within a state.

The train dates back to the 1920s, when the railway authorities introduced an especially comfortable connexion to and from Cape Town for the passengers of the Mail Ships that sailed backwards and forwards between South Africa and England. Another factor was that the South African government resided in northerly Pretoria, while parliament sat in Cape Town in the south. Civil servants and Members of Parliament obliged to commute between the two naturally welcomed this comfortable mode of transport.

In 1927 the standard sleeping coaches used till then by the "Union Limited" and the "Union Express" were replaced by special coaches. Shortly before the outbreak of World War II even more comfortable, air-conditioned sleepers, dining cars and saloon cars were delivered from England, only to be stored away until after the war. In 1946 the newly christened "Blue Train" made its first voyage.

The Mail boats stopped sailing years ago; state employees and the people's representatives have long since used the plane and make the journey from Cape Town to Johannesburg in two hours instead of the twenty-four and a half hours the Blue Train takes for the same strech (twenty-six for the entire journey of 1,005 miles from Cape Town to Pretoria). The passengers enjoy the journey like a luxury cruise on rails – and don't have to put their hands so deep in their pockets. The South African Railways admit that the Blue Train is a show-piece that they subsidize. Lunch and dinner as described above and a copious breakfast are all included in the price of the ticket.

The two trains now in use began their service in 1972, and the railway company is proud that every part was made in South Africa. Each train consists of 16 air-conditioned coaches – 11 sleeping cars, a saloon with bar, a dining car, kitchen, luggage wagon und a power-car that could supply a middle-sized town with electricity. Each train can carry up to 106 passengers, though normally they only take 92 so that everybody can be accommodated in the 46-seat dining-car in two sittings.

Travellers in the Standard Class have a choice between spacious single, double or three-bed compartments and "only" have community showers and toilets. In the Semi Deluxe Class there are single and three-bed compartments each with a private shower and toilet. However, unless a family occupies the compartment, normally only two passengers are assigned to the three-bed version. In the Deluxe class there is one three-bed and one single compartment each with a private bathroom, bath and toilet in both trains. The last word in railway luxury is the Super Deluxe apartment with its own lounge, bedroom with two separate beds, and a bathroom. The train has to stop twice en route to take on water as so much is used for baths and showers.

The Blue Train leaves Johannesburg Central station at 11.30 on the dot and speeds through the unchanging countryside of the Transvaal High Veld. After the passengers have settled in, they meet in the saloon for an aperitif. Most of them are dressed in casual clothes, for an unwritten law compels the majority of passengers to change for dinner as on a cruise – dinner being, of course, preceded by the customary South African "Sun Downer" at the bar.

In the night the train crosses the semi-desert of the Great Karoo, its pneumatically sprung swivel-chassis rocking the travellers to sleep. It must be remembered that the coaches are not mounted on the standard 57″ gauge but on the 42″ track that was employed by the British along the Cape route because of the topographical difficulties. Despite the narrow gauge the Blue Train reaches speeds of 70 mph.

The next morning, after a good night's rest, you touch a lever on the control panel beneath the sun-toned window silently raising the blinds, clean your teeth with iced water that gushes out of a special tap on the washbasin, take your newly-cleaned shoes out of a box under the bed, where they were put early in the morning through a hatch in the corridor by the steward. If you like to be cheerful in the mornings, you can choose between two radio programmes, in English or Afrikaans, or play taped music, when it is quite possible that you'll get the latest from the U.K. hit parade. All the knobs are on the control panel, which, incidentally, has instructions in the most frequently used international languages.

Breakfast naturally includes fruit juice, boiled, scrambled or fried eggs, toast, jam, marmelade, or honey, coffee or tea. And if you really want to got your money's worth, you can also order pancakes, fish, or even sausages and mash.

On the final stretch the train passes through Cape Province with its colourful mountain ranges and valleys. Around 11 o'clock many of the passengers go into the saloon for a farewell drink, for at 1 pm the train rolls into Cape Town Central in full view of Table Mountain. It is probably no exaggeration when the South African Railways contend that their costly show-piece has given the passengers the most luxurious train journey they will ever make. Hopefully, an experience that many tourists from all over the world will be able to enjoy, since the South African railways are considering the idea of introducing a new "Blue Train" in 1990.

South Africa's 25,000 year old Rock Paintings and Engravings – Who were the Artists?

It is generally known that cave drawings and paintings in Europa date back some 20,000 years.

Reports have also been heard about large numbers of drawings and engravings on rocks in north Africa in the area between the Atlantic and the Nile, as well as from the Sahara Highlands.

However, few people are aware that the finest and most expressive prehistoric paintings and imprints are to be found in the southern half of Africa – a veritable "open air museum" of African stone age art. New discoveries are constantly being made in what is today the South African provinces of Natal, Transvaal, Orange Free State and Cape Province. A further concentration of splendid drawings is known to be in the west of Namibia (South West Africa). Alone in the mountain slopes near Twyfelfontein, Brandberg, Kamanjab, Erongo, Spitzkoppe, the Khomas Highlands and Naukluft along the east edge of the Namib desert 15,000 engravings and 20,000 paintings have been found, and in South Africa there are at least as many again. "Rock art" – as it is called – is airily attributed to the aboriginal inhabitants of southern Africa, the hunting and gathering race of "Bushmen" (cf. the essay entitled "Peoples – But not a People" on page 68), but gradually this theory is becoming scientifically controversial. The age of the oldest painted rocks found in South West Africa north of the river Orange has been estimated at 25,000 years, while the most recent from the mountains in the west of Namibia are between 1,000 and 3,000 years old. Since the rock art in both South Africa and Namibia is identical in many phases, the question arises whether the Bushmen – today regarded as flatland dwellers – actually lived in the mountains in the far west of the land at that period. Maybe other, unknown races of hunters wandered across southern Africa, and their artistry is connected with the paintings of the Sahara or Nile civilizations. The present day Dama tribes (the Mountain Dama), on whose territory the most copious collection of rock art has been found, utterly refuse to be related to any unknown race of artists in any manner; for them the illustrations are a part of divine creation. It may therefore take some time before scientists are able to answer this question satifactorily – if ever. Basically, there are two types of rock art – paintings and engravings. The engravings have mostly been scratched or formed with sharp-edged stone tools into exterior rock faces. The subjects whose shape and movements have been excellently reproduced are predominantly those animals that were important to the artists as a source of food. Kudus with their unmistakeable screw-shaped horns, springboks, giraffes, zebras, rhinoceroses, elephants and oryx antelopes are expressively depicted in hunting scenes or shown, full size, in life-like flight. Scenes and friezes are often surrounded by abstract shapes like circles, snake-lines, and diamonds, the significance of which is still unknown. It is apparent that rock art is found almost exclusively in places where game migrated

on account of the favourable drinking or grazing conditions that were existent at the time. The question must be asked, why did these unknown hunters reproduce picture after picture of animals and hunting scenes? Perhaps they wanted to placate spiritual forces by bringing the game they had killed back to life in drawings. Or did they hope to create favourable conditions for future hunts? Similar lines of thought can still be traced in the ancient legends and tales of the old hunter tribes in southern Africa.

The paintings, for the greater part in caves or in the sheltered overhangs of cliffs, are much harder to find. The thousands of year-old colours have kept exceptionally well. Examination has shown that, in addition to mineral and vegetable paints, a durable mixture of lime and blood was used. As well as animals, people also figure frequently in the paintings, portrayed in the various poses of life. Hunting weapons, hair styles, clothing, jewellery and body paintings are all recorded in rich variety. Moreover, animal spirits, legendary figures and magical beings can be recognized, even though their meaning has remained unclear up to the present day. It is left to each observer to use his imagination.

Here is a brief selection of the most interesting cave drawings and engravings in **Namibia** and **South Africa.**

Namibia:
Twyfelfontein – 2,500 magnificent engravings including the great polished female kudu.

Tsisab Gorge in Brandberg – famous "White Lady" grotto, artistically the most valid cliff painting in southern Africa. In "Bushman paradise".

Great Spitzkoppe – many paintings of animals and spirits; particularly worth seeing is the "Rhinoceros Grotto".

Minor Spitzkoppe – "Ghost cave" (bird ghosts)

Erongo – Paintings around the Ameib farm. Specially interesting: the "Philipp Grotto" with large portrayals of animals.

Kamanjab – 1,500 splendid engravings, the biggest of which is a 10-foot tall giraffe.

South Africa:
Most of the sites of rock art are in Drakensberg in Natal in nature reserves, e.g.

– Giant's Castle game reserve
– Royal Natal National Park
– or in the vicinity of various hotels, guest farms or holiday resorts, such as:
– Boesmansnek Hotel, Cathedral Peak Hotel, Cathkin Park Hotel, Cavern Guest Farm, Dragens Peak Caravan Park, Drakensberg Garden Hotel, Solitude Mountain Resort, Sani Pass Hotel, Underberg Hotel.
Several of the establishments listed offer tours to the sites on foot, horse or by Landrover.

In addition, there are good collections of engravings or copies in
– Transvaal Museum, Pretoria
– Rock Art Museum, Johannesburg (Zoo)
– South African Museum, Cape Town
– National Museum, Blomfontein
– Museum Port Elizabeth (paintings)
– Museum Grahamstown (paintings)
– Museum Pietermaritzburg (paintings)
– Africana Museum, Johannesburg (paintings)   (TAR)

A few Words about the following Pages

As a place to spend a holiday, South Africa is unusual. Its favourable geographical position and climate are unusual. The variety of its countryside and natural wonders is unusual. The high quality of its roads, transport facilities and hotels is unusual. But its political situation is also unusual.

No one intending to visit South Africa can remain indifferent, for, from the very first moment one sets foot in this country, one is beset by its politics. The manner in which whites and non-whites live together – or rather side by side – will move, astound or even arouse depending on one's attitude and temperament. On the other hand, one may be surprised that there are hotels and restaurants where blacks and whites can live and eat under one roof. Is this an indication that "apartheid" – the main pinion of South African politics – is breaking up? Minor reforms have certainly already waived some of the so-called "minor apartheid", but steps that go beyond that are still a long way off.

If a holiday guide takes its task of helping to prepare and complete a holiday seriously – and this one does – then in the case of South Africa it must cover the political aspects, too. Such a guide, though, is not a political text-book that is obliged to trace in detail the historical development, to explain the current situation with all its ramifications, and to speculate about the future of South Africa, but rather to concern itself with supplying facts and figures devoid of opinion or criticism. Should you find the subsequent background information insufficient – and by the very nature of this guide it will have to be limited – then your attention is drawn to the reading list on page 138 that recommends not only literature of a purely touristic nature.

(Eicke)

The Course of History

Up to the 15th century, people in Europe knew practically nothing about southern Africa – and probably not particularly interested. For it must have appeared too arduous and unrewarding to leave the familiar strip of coast in the north of Africa to explore unknown territories in the south. The southern tip of Africa was believed to be unimaginably remote and secluded. Only the crews of isolated ships sailing along the south shores had observed small groups of dark-skinned hunters and nomads roaming through southern Africa. Today we know that these "aboriginal inhabitants" were the small Bushmen belonging to the old Sansan race and interrelated Hottentots (Khoikhio). The black Bantu tribes later penetrated from the north and drove them out of their hunting grounds along the coast. They withdrew westwards into the inhospitable interior. Nowadays a few small groups still live in Namibia together with various Bantu tribes, who also go to make up the black South African population.

300 hundred years of tumultuous South African history began in the 17th century, when the first whites in the service of the Dutch East India Company established a supply depot for merchant ships in what is today Cape Town. The Dutch settlers in the "Cape of Good Hope" were soon followed by French Huguenots and even some German emigrants. The result of the intermarriages between the Europeans and the Malays or the slaves brought from east and west Africa to the Cape was a race of half-breeds – the Coloureds – most of whose descendants still live in this region.

White meets black. Soon the white settlers needed more pasture for their cattle and pushed farther eastwards where they were confronted by groups of black "immigrants", members of the Bantu nation. A large contingent had left their overcrowded, tribal territory to seek new living space along the east coast. Just like the whites they laid claim to land for their livestock, but the European system of defined boundaries was new to them and they refused to accept it. The outcome was disputes and armed conflicts that lasted up to the beginning of the 20th century.

White vs white – black vs black. At the start of the 19th century the British took control of the Cape away from the Dutch and brought their colonialists into the country, arousing bitter reaction amongst the Dutch settlers (the Boers). Finally, in the face of deteriorating economic conditions in the Cape, the Boers were forced to capitulate and in the 1830s went on the "Long Trek", firstly, to the east and later northwards to the interior. At roughly the same time an abrupt radical upheaval took place among the black nations that was accompanied by population shifts and violent encroachments. This transformation was set off by the Zulus under the belligerent King Chaka, whose ruthless land-grabbing did not spare any of his black neighbours. At the memorable battle of Blood River in 1838, the out-numbered "Voortrekkers" beat the Zulus under the command of Dingaan, Chaka's successor. The Boers took this unexpected victory as a God-given omen. The Voortrekker Memorial in Pretoria is a stone reminder of this event.

The newly-founded state of Natal was annexed shortly after by the British for strategic reasons. They laid down sugar plantations and brought Indians into the country to work. Today the Indians represent the biggest group of Asians in South Africa and live mainly in Natal.

Further north the Boers founded the republics of the Orange Free State and Transvaal. Now the South African provinces of the same name are important centres of an economically powerful South Africa, whose wealth is based on rich natural resources.

The discovery of gold and diamonds in the latter part of the 19th century caused dramatic changes in the economical and political structure of South Africa. What had previously been an agricultural country became industrialized. Struggles for possession and power amongst the Europeans led to the two Boer Wars that put an end to the political independence of the Boers. But many of the black inhabitants lost the right to their home territories as well; advancing industrialization forced them into the role of itinerant workers and their homes were decreed by law.

White supremacy. When the British and Dutch territories were united under the sovereignty of the crown in 1910, no provision was made for non-whites to participate in politics. In the new Dominion the right to vote was reserved exclusively for the whites. The Boers became more and more immersed in politics, while the British concentrated more on commerce, so that under the Boer Presidents Lois Botha, Jan Christiaan Smuts and James B. M. Hertzog the tendency was more and more towards racial segregation. In 1931 South Africa became a sovereign state within the Commonwealth with the right to direct its own foreign policy. Under Smuts – once more Prime Minister after a break of 15 years – the country entered the Second World War on the side of the allies against the will of the Boers and experienced its greatest economic boom. In 1949–50 Dr. D. F. Malan, Smuts' successor, legalized apartheid, thereby provoking the first black revolts. The manner in which these were suppressed laid the ground-stone for South Africa's image as a racist state.

In 1961 the Union broke completely away from the mother country and the Republic of South Africa was born.

The 330 year "young" history of South Africa and its 24 million citizens has always been full of emotion. As in the recent past, so will the future be governed by the anxious question: Quo vadis, South Africa?

(TAR)

History at a Glance

1487 Bartholomaeus Diaz discovered the Cape of Good Hope
1652 In the name of the Dutch East India Company, Jan van Riebeeck established the first European settlement on the Cape – later to become Cape Town.
1688 Arrival of the first Huguenots. Wine-growing intensified
18th century Settlers penetrate north and east
1779 First confrontations between settlers and Bantus. Start of the Kafir Wars lasting a hundred years
1780–83 End of Dutch East India Company
1795–1803 First English occupation of the Cape
1803–1806 The Cape becomes part of the Batavian Republic
1809 Second English occupation of the Cape
1814 The Netherlands cede the Cape to Britain, who makes it a Crown Colony
1820 Arrival of 5,000 English settlers
1836 Start of the Great Trek
1839 The Voortrekkers found the first Boer republic – Natal
1843 England annexes Natal and declares it a Crown Colony
1852 and **1854** Founding of the Boer republics of Orange Free State and Transvaal and recognition by Britain
1860 First Indian workers land in Natal
1866 Diamonds discovered near Kimberley

1877 Transvaal annexed in the name of the Crown
1880–81 First Boer War. Re-establishment of an independent Transvaal under Paul (Oom) Kruger
1884 South West Africa becomes German protectorate
1886 Gold found at Witwatersrand. Founding of Johannesburg
1899–1902 Second Boer War. Defeat of Boers. Transvaal and Orange Free State declared British colonies.
1910 Proclamation of Union of South Africa as a Dominion of the British Empire
1919 Following World War I, the Union of South Africa is granted mandate by League of Nations for administration of South West Africa
1931 South Africa becomes sovereign state within the Commonwealth with own foreign policy
1939–45 Union of South Africa fights World War II on side of the Allies.
1961 South Africa opts out of Commonwealth and becomes a republic
1966 Lesotho and Botswana become independent
1967 Professor Barnard performs the world's first heart transplant in Cape Town
1968 Swaziland gains independence
Transkei granted independence in **1976,** Bophuthatswana in **1977,** Venda in **1979** and Ciskei in **1981;** all without international recognition.

South Africa today

The Republic of South Africa is regarded as the "last white bastion" in Africa and is the only country in the continent with a white government. Since the whites only represent a fifth of the South African population, a racial minority rules. This is the result of an historical, i. e. colonial development, that merged ethnic groups with dissimilar skin colours and origins – see the chapter entitled "Peoples – yet not a People". Still, every South African government since 1948 has only recognized two groups of people – whites and non-whites. For them the political principle of racial segregation, defined as "separate development" and better known as "Apartheid", holds true. This policy not only determines the relationship between whites and non-whites (mainly between whites and blacks), but also between the non-white groups – blacks, coloureds and Asians. The legal basis is a series of Acts, the first of which, the Native Urban Areas Act, was passed as early as 1923 regulating the separation of blacks and whites in urban districts. This was the beginning of the black townships, symbolized today by Soweto – South Western Townships – just outside Johannesburg. Subsequent Acts forbade marriage and intercourse between members of different races, disallowed non-whites (with the exception of the mixed bloods in Cape Province) the right to vote and regulated service contracts for the African natives.

Of far-reaching significance were two Acts passed at the beginning of the 1950s: The Group Areas Act and The Bantustan Authorities Act. They ordered that every South African be classified by race and allocated to a race-related living area. This went hand in hand with a law ordering the re-settlement of non-whites into "Homelands" that have since been granted independence by South Africa: Transkei 1976, Bophuthatswana 1977, Venda 1979 and Ciskei 1981. Together with their new Homeland nationality, the blacks – large numbers of whom had been living in the towns – acquired the status of foreign or itinerant workers whose right to work or reside outside their ascribed Homeland or self-governing state was limited in time and revocable. Only about half of the black population – called "Natives" – actually live and work in the Homelands. Of the rest, those who do not reside in the cities work in neighbouring or white rural areas.

Hardly less complex than the ethnic and political situation is the economic and social one, as can be judged by the preceding comments. Another of several aspects – albeit a very important one – is the fact that, thanks to its rich natural resources, South Africa is one of the world's leading suppliers of raw materials. It holds top rank in the international list of exports for gold, chrome, platinum and vanadium. In mining, as in other branches of industry, the better educated whites occupy most of the managerial positions, while the unskilled and semi-skilled jobs are in the main filled by the blacks. Consequently, the white population enjoys a high western standard of living, while the black sector is more on a par with the standards of the Third World. Despite considerable improvements in educational facilities for the blacks over the past years, wages that have increased two and a half times quicker than for whites, and the practical elimination of "job reservations" the discrepancy between the living standards is not likely to alter much for the time being. Nor is the situation of workers having to live away from their families in the Homelands. Once a year they receive a long paid holiday, but are not allowed to bring their families to live with them at their place of employment.

Peoples – yet not a People

This sums up the complexity, and the tragedy, of South Africa. The population is comprised of four main racial groups, each consisting of different peoples partially with their own cultural and ethnic identity and having little in common, while that which distinguishes is obvious for all to see – the colour of their skin.

The Blacks
The first who drifted from the over-populated areas of the north into what is now South Africa were more dark brown than black; the small shrivel-skinned Bushmen with their typically short tightly-curled hair lying close to the scalp belong – together with the Pygmies – to the ancient Sansan race. They lived in small groups and, in spite of having only simple weapons, were excellent hunters. Permanent huts or encampments were unknown to them. Sheltered from the elements in hollows or under primitive wind-breakers they lived like their Stone Age ancestors. Yet the splendid rock and cave paintings found mainly in the southern part of Cape Province and

Namibia are attributed to this race, although recent datings put some of these paintings at a considerably older period, so that it is less certain who the artists were. The Bushmen have a unique and peculiar click-filled language that has been partially adopted by the related Hottentots (Khoikhoi). Both groups – collectively called Khoisanide – later had to leave the area under the increasing pressure of the nomadic black Bantu tribes who took possession of the land for their sheep and cattle. Armed with iron weapons they were vastly superior to the Bushmen and drove them westwards. Today Bushmen and Hottentots form a minority in Botswana and Namibia.

The Sotho branch of the Bantu nation with its main tribe, the Tswana, settled in the north and centre of the country, while the Nguni branch (Zulus, Swazi and Xhosa) spread out along the east coast in what is today the Province of Natal and Transkei. Unlike the Nguni, the Sotho established permanent villages and even sizable towns on their way south. A parallel exists in north-easterly Zimbabwe, where a mighty and prosperous kingdom dwelt in a city made of granite. Metals such as copper and gold mined in Zimbabwe were traded with Arab countries.

No matter which branch they belonged to, the Bantu nations all lived in compact tribes with a ruling class and a set of strict tribal rules; for example, if a tribe was in danger of out-growing its optimum size, the son of the chief chose a young team and went in search of new living space. For the Bantu, livestock is synonymous with vitality and was only devoured in sacred form. Superstition and the belief in spirits played an important role and the medicine-man excercised a considerable influence in all decisions and actions within the tribe. This has carried through to the present day, though in a milder form.

The Bantu nations still have very much in common: polygamy is legal; the family means more to the individual than in European society; members of the tribe are not considered adult until married, and parents still have a say in the choice of partner. The oft misunderstood concept of bride-buying compensates the bride's father and assures the bride's financial standing. The groom can always count on financial support from his relations, even more so as the number of wives and children are a status symbol of the Bantu warrior.

Typical for the Bantu are the strong family ties; for example, brothers are equal in all respects and, if need be, can take each

other's place as father and even as husband. The chain of authority keeps offspring close to tribe and family, and the practice of one member working to keep the whole family is a part of this system.

The family net of the Bantu is wide-spread and closely-knit, even uncles and aunts count as blood relatives with all resultant obligations for the duty-bound individual. That is why so many blacks who work in the towns are compelled to break connexions with the family in the Homelands and to duck out of sight – which is why they are so furious about the registration laws. It is only a matter of time before the traditional structure of Bantu society dies out.

The Coloureds

This group of mixed bloods breaks down into two groups: the Griquas whose forebears were whites and Hottentots and who live for the greater part in the northern part of Cape Province, and the Cape Malays, descendants of Muslim slaves brought into the country by the Dutch, who have made their home around Cape Town. The Coloureds look upon themselves as belonging to the "white" half of society, but are economically and socially underprivileged. So high is their birthrate that 45% are under 15. The 2.5 million Coloureds, whose mother-tongue is mostly Afrikaans, have grown to be a political force that ought to be under-estimated. They regard the racial discrimination against them as indefensible and historically unfounded. Indeed, they argue that they are the true South Africans,

The British in South Africa

The first Englishman to see the shores of what later became South Africa wrote: "This Cape is the most stately thing, and the fairest cape we saw in the whole circumference of the earth". The year was 1580 and the writer Sir Francis Drake. His words are often quoted and possibly many visitors arriving on the passenger liner service from Britain have the same kind of thoughts when they round the Cape.

The Cape was colonized by the Dutch in the 17th century and they, and a sprinkling of Huguenot refugees, populated the region in the first 150 years. The only British at that time were botanists like Francis Masson who went to collect plants and bulbs for Kew Gardens in 1771 and spent 12 years studying the fascinating flora.

In 1795 half of Europa was at war with the young French Republic and rather than risk having the Cape fall into French hands, the British moved in and remained there until 1803 when they put control into the hands of the Batavian Republic. In 1806 the British retook the Cape and from then until the formation of the Union of South Africa in 1910 the Cape and Natal became British colonies. The interior was opened up by Dutch settlers dissatisfied with life at the Cape under British rule and took the form of two independent Republics – the Transvaal and the Orange Free State.

From now on British ascendancy was complete. Governors and administrators, doctors and missionaries, adventurers and entrepreneurs came from England, Scotland and Ireland. The first organized immigration of British settlers took place in 1820 when 4,500 were landed at Algoa Bay (now Port Elizabeth) to develop what was then frontier country. Soon afterwards a settlement was made at Port Natal (now Durban) by a group of English traders who managed to make friends with the otherwise tyrannical leader of the Zulus, Shaka. From the 1840s onward British immigrants moved into Natal which is still the most Anglicized of the four provinces. The next important development in the story of the British in South Africa was the discovery of diamonds at Kimberley in 1872. This event attracted adventurers from all over the world including a large proportion of footloose British in search of their fortunes. The diamond fields also threw up names that came to be of great importance to the future of the country: Cecil Rhodes, Dr. Jameson, Barney Barnato – three Englishmen who dominated the scene for years to come. Cecil Rhodes, by far the greatest of the trio, consolidated the diamond diggings at the "Big Hole" in Kimberley, then moved on to the goldfields of the Witwatersrand in the 1880s and later gave his name to Rhodesia – now of course Zimbabwe.

Dr. Jameson was his doctor and friend at Kimberley and was later tacitly authorized by Rhodes to invade the Transvaal Republic in an attempt to redress the grievances of the foreigners working on the goldfields who claimed they were given no say in the running of their adopted country and who hoped to force reforms on the immutable president, Paul Kruger. The raid proved a failure and Rhodes was reproved by a British parliamentary select committee. When Rhodes died five years later he left vast tracts of land on and around Table Mountain to the nation and instituted the Rhodes Scholarship scheme which continues to benefit suitable young men, mostly from the English-speaking world, who are subsidised to attend Oxford University.

The "Jameson Raid" was one of the events that led to the Boer War of 1899–1902 when a large contingent of British troops was required to beat the skilful but outnumbered Boer Commandos. However, the British proved generous victors and within eight years of the peace treaty the Union of South Africa had been set up as an independent self-governing dominion within the Commonwealth.

At this time South Africa was breeding its own heroes and leaders of both British and Afrikaner stock, though immigration from Britain continued, reaching a peak from 1947 to 1949 when 50,000 arrived. Despite this influx, Afrikaans is the mother tongue of more than half the white population – both Afrikaans and English are the official languages of the Republic.

As a generalization one could say the English influence in South Africa has been technological and commercial whereas the Afrikaner has historically been a man of the land. However, these generalities are breaking down as new generations take on new roles in a land where the white population becomes more united year by year.

since their breed was created in this country.

The Asians

The most powerful element in this group are the Indians who can be divided up into different linguistic and religious sections. Initially they came as workers on the sugar plantations in Natal during the middle of the 19th century.

Once their contracts ran out they were given the choice of returning home to India or buying land from the crown. The majority stayed and became shopkeepers, artisans, farmers or went into business. 85% of the Indians live in Natal around Durban. The remainder has settled in the industrial areas of Johannesburg and Pretoria. They have adhered to their handed-down traditions and religion, so that 70% still follow the official Indian religion – Hinduism – and 20% are Moslems. The Indians have done well commercially and socially in South Africa and have been accepted in the professions. They keep themselves to themselves and have strong family ties. But they are by no means liked by the black population, and so they find themselves in a paradoxical situation: on the one hand they suffer under the racial policies of the white minority, yet they fear nothing more than black participation in the government or a take-over of power by the blacks. Their efforts go towards achieving a multi-racial form of government. A second, smaller group of Asians are the Chinese who were encouraged to come and work in the mines in the Transvaal at the end of the 19th century, when it was more difficult to get "natives". About 50,000 – mostly coolies – left their homes in the province of Shantung and emigrated to South Africa where many of them stayed, later attracting others. Some of the Chinese who came belonged to the higher social ranks and eventually became successful in the gold and diamond trade.

The Whites

Two groups dominate the white population in South Africa and are best identified by their languages – English and Afrikaans. Afrikaans is derived from Dutch and is the mother tongue of all those who consider South Africa **their** country, **their** native soil and consider themselves Afrikaners. They are not only descendants of the Dutch settlers, who made their home in the Cape after 1652, but also of the Huguenots and Germans who followed. English is spoken by the heirs of the colonialists and pioneers sent after 1820 by the crown to take possession of conquered Boer territory. In many respects they associate themselves more with the mother country than with their present home in southern Africa. As a result of intensive intermingling of both groups a new identity has emerged and many prefer to call themselves "South Africans". Officially, South Africa is bilingual and both languages are compulsory in school – but this does not prevent the other language from being "foreign". In addition to English and Afrikaans there are other languages and, therefore, other national groups. Of these, German – on account of the one-time colony of South West Africa – is the most important, followed by Portuguese (from the former colonies of Angola Mozambique), Italian, Greek, French and Yiddish. Although these national groups preserve their own cultural heritage, they have all contributed something to the South African way-of-life.

South Africa – Product of Two Oceans

Africa is jammed between the Atlantic and the Indian Ocean like a gigantic wedge, and both oceans meet where the landmass comes to a spectacular culmination – the Cape of Good Hope.

The waves that wash against the cliffs in an eternal rhythm do not reveal that they are a mixture of two completely contrary currents: the warm Mozambique-Agulhas Current originating in the equatorial region of the Indian Ocean, and the cold Benguela Current from the Antarctic. Strange though it may sound, over millions of years these two ocean streams have made southern Africa what it is; have formed the landscape, the life of people, plants and animals, and have even influenced the historical development. The difference in their temperatures accounts for the astonishing contrast in climate and character of various parts of the country – from swamps and jungle to savannah, prairie and desert.

The tropically warm Mozambique Current, with water temperatures of approximately 24°C (75°F) between May and August and 28°C (82°F) from October to February, is responsible for the subtropical climate and vegetation along the coast of Natal. The lush greenery of this coastal strip is a direct result of the high amount of condensation from the warm sea and the consequent rainfall.

As it progresses southwards along the coast the Mozambique Current cools down and is only 18°C–20°C (65°F–68°F) by the time it reaches the Cape Peninsula, thus explaining the moderate mediterranean type climate of the western Cape.

The Benguela Current, coming from the Antarctic and cooled by icebergs and the deep waters of the polar sea, reaches the southern tip of Africa with a temperature of only 10°C (50°F), meets the Mozambique Current head-on and is deflected northwards, where it flows along the west coast of Africa up to the equator. Its effect on climate and vegetation is not nearly as pleasant as its counterpart in the east. Not even the intense African sun can ring condensation out of this frosty block of water, so that no rain clouds are formed. The outcome is that the coast is afflicted by permanent drought, as witnessed by the 900 mile long Namib Desert between the mouth of the river Orange in the south and the border with Angola in the north. Wind and sun have done the rest to create a unique sea of sand with dunes up to 1,000 feet high – one of the most fascinating deserts on earth.

In this way the currents from two oceans excercise a decisive influence over an area that – even if we only take South Africa and Namibia – covers 800,000 square miles, an area eight times the size of the United Kingdom. This has brought about an almost unimaginable varie-

— Average annual temperature at ocean surface

Cold stream   Warm stream

Equator

27°C
24°C

21°C

24°C

18°C

21°C
18°C

15°C

15°C
13°C

13°C

10°C

10°C

7°C

7°C

4°C

0   400km
0   250 miles

ty of landscapes and living conditions that accommodate a rich selection of animals and plants unequalled throughout the dark continent.

If you are susceptible to the infinite beauty of nature, then South Africa will fill you with happy experiences and impressions.

Position and Landscape

"South Africa" is an expression that is frequently used in a way that causes uncertainty and misunderstanding, for there is a considerable difference whether one is referring to the geographical area or the political one, i. e. the Republic of South Africa. So this chapter begins with a definition.

By "southern Africa" we mean that immense area in the southern half of the African continent that lies between the Cunene river at the frontier separating Angola and Namibia and the Zambesi river that divides Zambia and Zimbabwe, and between the Atlantic and Indian oceans. By "South Africa" we shall be referring to the Republic of South Africa. These concepts will be employed in the following explanations. (In other cases, for example when writing about animals and plants, it is not always possible to adhere to them strictly.)

South Africa is, therefore, a part of southern Africa, but – to start at the beginning – how big a part? This question probably seems as strange as the answer itself; the state of South Africa is getting smaller all the time. Every time a Homeland is granted independence the surface area and the population disappear

from South Africa's statistics. This will be discussed later.

If we take the statistics for 1983, the country covered an area of 436,200 square miles – the equivalent of the United Kingdom, France, Germany and Italy together. By the way, the distances are also comparable, an important factor when travelling by car or mobile home. From Pretoria to Cape Town it is almost 940 miles – about as far as London to Madrid – and from Cape Town to Durban 1,100, or something like London to Rome.

More comparisons: Cape Town lies 1,800 miles below the equator on the same latitude as Buenos Aires and Sydney. Extending this distance north of the equator we arrive at Cyprus, Casablanca or San Diego in California. This gives an idea of what South Africa has in store for you climatically. The country lies almost entirely within the moderate zone of southern Africa. The Tropic of Capricorn runs through the northern part of Transvaal, so that only a few thousand square miles of the Republic are in the Tropics. More about this in the chapter on "Climate".

Two of the four South African provinces – Transvaal with 100,000 square miles and the Orange Free

State with 49,000 square miles – have no access to the sea. The other two – Cape Province (252,000 square miles) and Natal (33,500 square miles) – share the 950 mile long coastline at an unequal ratio of 3 : 1. Unequal but not unfair, since touristically the west coast is rendered virtually unusable by the cold Antartic Benguela Current. Bathers are much better off in the Mozambique Current in Natal on the east side.

But that's enough figures and comparisons. What does South Africa really look like? Firstly, one must understand the topography – that is, the surface – and here an image will help. Seen from a satellite the country would resemble an up-turned saucer. In the centre a wide plateau, the High Veld, between 3,000 and 6,000 feet (average 4,000 ft) above sea level and predominantly a treeless prairie. In the north it falls away as Bush towards the Limpopo plain – a typical savannah region with high grass and spasmodic trees. In the west and southwest it is met by the dry, steppe-like country of the Bushmen and the Great Karoo right up to the Great Escarpment. This is a natural borderline between the highland and the coastal area; a chain of mountains stretching like an enormous horseshoe from north-east Transvaal along the east and south coast to Namaqualand in the west. The escarpment often only leaves a narrow strip of fertile pastures with rivers and streams in the east and south and a belt of semi-desert in the west. Solely in the south-west is the transition less abrupt, dropping away in several step-like terraces: the Great Escarpment is followed by the Great Karoo with elevations between 2,000 and 3,000 feet as far as the Swartberg mountains. From there unfolds the Little Karoo with an average height of 1,500 feet reaching to the Langeberg mountains. Both are dry regions bearing the shrubs and gorse that is typical of the Karoo.

In the north-east the foreland reveals a special feature – the Low Veld between the escarpment and the Lebombo mountains, which also form the border with Mozambique. The flat savannah plateau, some 600 feet above sea level and covered with bushes, sparse trees, river beds and hills, is almost identical with the Kruger National Park, making it ecologically uniform.

In general, a survey of the South African countryside leaves an impression of disunity, or – to put it in positive terms – variety. This will be to your advantage when planning your South African holiday, even more so, if you take into consideration the variations in climate.

Climate, Weather, Travel Times

South Africa lies in the southern hemisphere and its seasons are, naturally enough, diametrically opposed to the north. In July and August it is the middle of winter in South Africa. On the High Veld, which includes Johannesburg and Pretoria, this can mean nightly temperatures below freezing. Contrarily, one must be prepared to spend Christmas in the Kruger National Park in the Low Veld or on the beach in Natal suffering under a summerly 35 °C (95 °F).

However, it is not sufficient to merely ascertain that the seasons are opposite to ours. Just as here different parts of the country can have different weather at the same time of the year, so is this true of South Africa to a greater extent since the country is many times larger. But there is no need to worry about radical extremes, for South Africa is in the warm moderate subtropical zone. Two factors, above all, cause these differences: firstly, South Africa's east coast is washed by the warm Mozambique-Agulhas Current and its west coast by the cold Benguela Current. Secondly, 40% of the country is High Veld lying more than 4,000 feet above sea level, so that the temperature is several degrees lower than other regions on the same latitude.

In the southern winter a fairly stable high pressure zone determines the climate of the interior. The High Veld and the northerly regions enjoy dry sunny weather, although the nights are cold with occasional frost. Only the narrow coastal belt and the Low Veld are spared this because of their lower altitude. At the same time the seasonal west winds form low pressure areas around the Cape bringing rain to the Cape Mountains, especially to Table Mountain, and making the west Cape the sole region in south Africa with winter rain. However, one

should not expect the violent and abundant rainstorms of the Tropics. The rain usually comes in gentle, though often prolonged, showers – just the way the subtropical vegetation and the Cape vines like it . . .

In summer an extensive zone of high pressure spreads over the Cape from the Atlantic to the Indian Ocean, bringing hot dry weather. Further east, along the coast of Natal, there is a corridor of warm moist air from the Indian Ocean that drifts westwards, dropping its moisture in heavy downpours or short sharp thunderstorms. Normally the summer rains last from January to March in Natal (notably in the holiday area around Durban) and reach a climax in January in the Transvaal. Between the winter rain region in the west Cape and the summer rain region in Natal lies a strip of coast where the precipitation is spread evenly over the whole year. It comes within 60–100 miles of Cape Town and East London, thus encompassing the entire "classical" section of the Garden Route from Mossel Bay to Port Elizabeth. The little rain that does come, however, falls mostly during the night.

The best times to travel vary from region to region, but the difference from the "best" time and a good, pleasant time is normally so minimal that one could say that any time is a good time to visit South Africa. Here are a few hints that will help you choose a suitable season.

The most agreeable time of the year to visit the Kruger National Park in east Transvaal, the various nature reserves in Natal and the beaches around Durban is during the southern winter from June through August – incidentally, coinciding with the main holiday period. As far as the Gemsbok National Park is concerned this winter period can be extended from March to October.

If you visit Johannesburg and Pretoria on the high plateau of the interior, then the summer months – September through March – are to be recommended. It is worth noting that the jacaranda blossoms in Pretoria between October and November. By the same token, you can expect dry sunny weather in the Cape during the southern summer. Statistics show that the number of sun hours reach a peak from November to February, whereby it should be added that the Cape literally outshines other well-known sun-spots like California, Florida and the Caribbean – Cape Town recording 298 days of sun annually.

For floral enthusiasts, spring is best. Several thousand types of daisy bloom in their millions in Namaqualand from August to September, while the Cape flora comes to full blossom at the same time.

The same period is recommended for the Garden Route for the same reason. Moreover, a trip in September and October can be combined with a swim in the Indian Ocean where the water remains warm right up till March.

For the **whole** of South Africa, April and May are regarded as the best and sunniest months – the summer rains are over and the period of winter rain in the Cape has not yet started.

The climate in Cape Town

Month	Daily high		Nightly low		Daily hours of sun-shine	Water-temp.		Hu-mid-ity	no. of days with rain
	°C	°F	°C	°F		°C	°F	in %	
January	26	79	16	60	12	18	64	54	4
February	26	79	16	60	10	19	66	54	3
March	25	77	14	57	9	19	66	57	4
April	22	72	12	54	8	18	64	60	8
May	20	68	10	50	6	17	63	65	9
June	18	64	8	46	6	16	61	64	10
July	17	63	7	45	6	15	69	67	11
August	18	64	8	46	7	14	57	65	11
September	19	66	9	48	8	15	59	62	7
October	21	70	11	52	9	16	61	58	7
November	23	73	13	55	10	17	63	56	3
December	25	77	14	57	11	18	64	54	4

The climate in Johannesburg

Month	Daily high		Nightly low		Daily hours of sun-shine	Hu-mid-ity in %	no. of days with rain
	°C	°F	°C	°F			
January	26	79	15	59	8	50	13
February	25	77	14	57	8	51	9
March	24	75	13	55	7	49	8
April	22	72	10	50	8	43	7
May	19	66	6	43	9	37	3
June	17	63	4	37	9	34	1
July	17	63	4	37	9	35	0
August	20	68	6	43	10	33	1
September	23	73	9	48	9	34	2
October	25	77	12	54	9	38	11
November	25	77	13	55	9	44	12
December	25	77	14	57	9	48	13

The climate in Durban

Month	Daily high		Nightly low		Daily hours of sun-shine	Water-temp.		Hu-mid-ity in %	no. of days with rain
	°C	°F	°C	°F		°C	°F		
January	27	80	21	70	6	24	75	72	9
February	28	82	21	70	7	24	75	73	8
March	27	80	20	68	6	24	75	74	9
April	26	79	18	64	7	23	73	71	7
May	24	75	14	57	7	22	72	66	4
June	23	73	12	54	7	21	70	61	3
July	22	72	11	52	7	21	70	61	3
August	22	72	13	55	7	20	68	68	4
September	23	73	15	59	6	21	70	71	7
October	24	75	17	63	5	21	70	73	10
November	25	77	18	64	6	22	72	74	11
December	26	79	20	68	6	23	73	73	10

South Africa – the economic Giant

South Africa's racial and internal problems are so much the focus of international attention that its importance as an economic power is often pushed into the background. Yet the country plays a key role not only for the African continent but for the economy of the entire western world.

Firstly, a few African perspectives. South Africa represents approx. five per cent of the population of the African continent and a fraction more than three per cent of its surface area. By comparison, the Republic accounts for 40% of the industrial production, 45% of the minerals mined, 64% of the electricity produced, 66% of the steel consumption, 41% of the maize grown, 18% of the wheat, almost 20% of the livestock and 25% of the GNP. Despite pursuing a policy of political isolation for South Africa for many years, a great number of black African states have continued to trade actively with the country. At the last count 49 African states were trading partners of South Africa. 70% of their imports from the Republic were for manufactured goods, but quite a few import basic food-stuffs – particularly maize – as well. South Africa is now the only country in the continent that can not only feed its own population, but can export food over and above that. Yet agricultural products are neither the most important export, nor the most important economic factor in South Africa. Their significance was reduced as two other branches – mining and industrial production – increased. This shift reflects South Africa's progression from an agricultural country in the 18th and 19th centuries, to a supplier of raw materials up to the end of World War I, and finally to industrial producer. Today manufactured goods hold top rank in the Gross National Product, closely followed by minerals – agriculture represents only one seventh of these two together.

For the non-African, preponderately western trading partners, South

79

Tourism

Despite all political antagonism tourism has reached respectable heights in South Africa. The numbers cannot, of course, be compared to the Mediterranean – the relatively long distances and high costs do not allow it – yet in 1981 a quarter of a million visitors came from Great Britain, USA and the rest of the European Community. The numbers of visitors from the latter two are more or less the same every year (1981: 57,000 Americans and 56,000 Europeans. The previous year: 49,000 and 50,000) and are easily exceeded by the British who, with 133,000 visitors, represent the largest contingent. However, it is estimated that 65%–70% of the British visit relatives and friends living in South Africa while the same percentage of Europeans are tourists in the true sense. Of the American and European tourists a sizable proportion are on repeat visits; about half are on their second, third or even fourth tour. Though many of these are politically sympathetic to the Republic, it also seems that a great many come back because the picture gained from a single visit was not enough for them to form an opinion. Many return because they are fascinated by the beauty and variety of the country and realise that it cannot all be taken in on a three week tour – the most popular stay.

According to South African statistics tourism in 1981 generated a revenue of 459 million Rand, but South Africans spent much more than this abroad. In view of an export volume of 34 billion Rand tourism contributes too little – although it does bring hard currency – to be listed as a significant industry. Nevertheless, the promotion of tourism has a high priority in the country, motivated by the wish to give people the opportunity to see South Africa as it really is and so improve the rather unflattering political image.

Africa's mineral production is far more important as these minerals are needed for military purposes. These include elements of the platinum group (platinum, palladium, rhodium, osmium, iridium and Ruthenium) of which South Africa has supplied 91% of the west's requirements since 1978. Similarly, South Africa holds 90% of the west's vanadium and can fulfil almost all its requirements. The list continues with 93% of the manganese deposits of the western world and 80% of the chrome. Finally, the country is one of the leading producer of uranium, a by-product of gold. Which brings us to those two minerals whose discovery in the sixties and seventies of the last century started South Africa's rise as an economic power – diamonds and gold. Currently South Africa extracts more dress diamonds than any other country in the world and produces 70% of the free world's gold – and it is this product that for years has been South Africa's biggest export.

Of all the natural deposits there is only one that the Republic does not possess – oil. Small finds have been made off the south and west shores, but South Africa's energy requirements will be dependant on coal for the foreseeable future, and this is available in more than sufficient quantities. The economically viable reserves total 26 billion tons, enough to last 200 years at the present rate of production. This includes those quantities that will be converted into liquid gas, for with European support they have built the only plant in the world, the SASOL installation, that can profitably convert coal into petrol and oil. The result will almost certainly be that the present preponderance of coal for energy requirements – at present 80%, and that mainly for power stations – will rise still further. In view of the uranium deposits in South Africa nuclear power stations will also become increasingly important. All this indicates a healthy modern state whose citizens enjoy a remarkable standard of living. But the appearance is deceptive. The privileges that the whites receive during their professional training and development mean that, primarily, they are the ones who profit from economic success. In fact about three quarters of the population have a below average share of the results because, due to their scanty earnings, they are unable to take advantage of the goods and services on offer. During your journey through South Africa you will become aware of the discrepan-

cy between the high western style of living of the white community and the Third World living standard in the black townships and in the country and it may give you cause to think. Although the government is making an obvious effort to give the "natives" a larger share of the benefits by improving education, increasing the job supply and minimalizing the disparity with the earnings of the whites, there is still a long way to go. South Africa's friends and partners can only hope that this will be accomplished without any turbulence that could dislocate the economic bulwark that is South Africa.

Palatable Pleasures

When Jan van Riebeeck hoisted the Dutch flag for the first time on south African soil in 1652 and founded Cape Town he became the forerunner of the many nutritious pleasures awaiting you in South Africa. Yet the setting up of the orchard and vegetable garden in the same year – now a botanical garden and a welcome sight offering an oasis of tranquillity in the centre of the city – had less culinary effect than another pioneering deed: in 1655 van Riebeeck planted the first vines originating from France, Spain and Germany on the Cape. Subsequently, on the 2nd February, 1659, he noted in his diary: "Praise God, today we were able to press the first wine out of grapes from the Cape."

The youthful South African wine culture received two more impulses shortly afterwards. Simon van der Stel, Riebeeck's successor as governor, had 100,000 vines planted in the Valley of Constantia in 1680 thereby laying the foundation for the first successful Cape wine. The Constantia dessert wine so pleased the nobles in the European courts that they preferred it to Port and Madeira. Finally, religiously persecuted Huguenots fled to South Africa in 1688 and their knowledge of the art of wine-making gave a powerful boost to wine production on the Cape.

It was not only the French but also German immigrants and their descendants who made the area around Stellenbosch and Paarl one of the most important regions in South Africa for growing quality wines. A tour of the wine-growing areas is to be recommended to all – not just connoisseurs. If you are pressed for time, you can join one of the one-day excursions that are offered in several variations by the travel agencies in Cape Town, or book with a UK travel company before departure. Trips are organised to well-known vineyards like "Nederburg" near Paarl and – if you lucky enough to be there, when they are not travelling – you may well meet some world-famous cellarmen.

Still, it is more rewarding to take a little more time and go under your own steam. As an individual traveller you will often receive an appreciative welcome in vineyards that do not have the facilities to entertain coaches, even though such visits often have to take place at set times or need to be announced beforehand by telephone. Further details are available from the local wine

The Wine Regions of South Africa

All of South Africa's vineyards are within a 100 mile radius of Cape Town. Thanks to the variety in the earth and climatic conditions this relatively limited area produces a range of wines that, in Europe, are grown in countries that are far apart.

In the coastal district of south-west Cape Province, are situated the classical wine-growing regions of Constantia, Durbanville, Paarl, Stellenbosch and Malmesbury. The Atlantic wind brings rain to this region in the winter; in the summer a breeze blows from the Indian Ocean keeping the vines cool and healthy. All in all, ideal conditions for growing the best quality red and white wines, not to mention excellent sherries, specifically around Paarl.

The fertile valley of the Breede River spreads out on the far side of the Drakenstein mountains in the direction of the Langeberg range, embracing such historical towns as Worcester, Robertson, Bonnievale and the district of Mantagu. The summers are hot with little rain, allowing dry whites, robust sherries and sweet wines to prosper.

On the east side of **the Little Karoo**, between the Langeberg and the Swartberg mountains, is a stretch of fairly dry unfertile land. Partly with the help of artificial irrigation, grapes are grown around Barrydale, Ladismith and the "ostrich capital", Oudtshoorn, that produce good table wines, sweet dessert wines and brandy, which holds a not unimportant place in the drinking habits of the South Africans and can stand every comparison with internationally recognised brandies.   *(TAR)*

South Africa's wine seal

The quality of the wine is indicated by the colour of the seal on the bottle-neck proving that it has been checked by the Wine and Spirit Board. A brief summary:

The word "Estate" means that the wine was grown on an officially registered vineyard.

The blue band ("origin") confirms that the wine has not been blended.

The red band guarantees the vintage shown on the label.

The green band guarantees that the wine was pressed from a specified type of grape.

The word "Superior" inside a golden seal has been in use since 1. 3. 82 to characterize a wine of exceptional quality.

Bobotie – Curried minced meat

900 grams (2 lbs) minced beef or mutton, 2 onions, 1 slice bread or roll, ½ pint milk, 2 eggs, 1 tablespoon curry powder, 1 tablespoon sugar, 2–3 teaspoons salt, ½ teaspoon pepper, pinch saffron (or more), 2 tablespoons vinegar or juice from 1 lemon, 6 quartered almonds, 125 grams (4 ozs) cored raisings, 4 bay leaves, 2 tablespoons mango chutney.

Slice onions and simmer till soft, chop into cubes and fry lightly. Soak bread or roll in milk and crumble. Work all ingredients, except 1 egg and bay leaves, together and transfer to large, flat, greased casserole. Roll bay leaves and distribute vertically over mixture. Bake for 30 minutes at 300 to 350°F (Gas Mark 2–3). Whisk remaining egg with a little milk and spread over mixture 10 minutes before removal. Serve hot with rice and chutney.

growers' associations. For example, if you are interested in visiting the Stellenbosch region: Cape Estate Wine Producers Association, Post Box 10, Koelenhof, Cape Province.

But the South Africans do not only swear by wine. Another drink is also very much – and this goes for the quantity too – in demand: beer. After all, one is attempting to master a local preference for hearty meals and this is a little easier with a light lager. This help is particularly welcome since the country is in the throes of barbecue-mania. Everything is celebrated with a "braai", making severe demands on the teeth. "Braai" is the popular abbreviation of braaivlies, which means "grilled over an open fire". To transform pork, beef, mutton and sausage (e. g. the spiral-shaped "boerewors" or country sausage) into gigantic crisp brown meals is both a favourite South African pastime and a social activity. As a guest you will be drawn into a braaivlies party spontaneously and heartily, whether it be in a private circle, a camping-site or the rest camp on a wildlife reservation.

Many nations have brought their cuisine and eating habits to South Africa: the Huguenots, the English, south and central Europeans. But none has contributed as much as the Malays who came to the Cape as slaves 300 years ago. A profusion of delectable dishes, some with modifications, are of Malay origin, such as "sosaties" (spiced mutton and pork meatballs on a skewer), "bobatie" (minced meat in curry) or various "bredie" (meat and vegetable stews).

You will be able to try out such specialities, primarily, in Cape Town, but they are on the menus of many good restaurants throughout the land. This is also true of another type of cooking to be found mainly around Durban – Indian. If you like curry dishes, then you can indulge in

all the variations – poultry, meat, fish, vegetable or egg curry –, hot or mild.

The coast can present a heavenly feast too: fish and lobster, referred to here as crayfish, and in a price range that enables it to be ordered more than once. By the way, "line-fish" is not a kind of fish but a definition for fresh fish, just off the line.

Another general term is "biltong", meaning dry meat. In the pioneering days it played an important role as an easily storable and transportable energy-giving food. Nowadays it serves as a snack and the meat can be kudu, ostrich or even elephant.

Biltong is also sold by street dealers and can be bought without hesitation. There is no need to worry about the cleanliness of food in the cities or in rural hotels and restaurants frequented by tourists.

You can drink water out of the tap and need not bother to fish the ice cubes out of your drink.

Talking of drinks, there are licensing laws in South Africa and alcohol can only be sold at certain times and only in specified combinations. For this reason watch for the following signs in hotels and restaurants:

Y = wine and beer can only be served with meals;
YY = only wine and beer can be served
YYY = wine, beer and spirits can be served.

Women are not allowed in bars or pubs anywhere in the country – not even in male company. This limitation does not apply to the lounge in licensed hotels. Some hotels have a "Ladies Lounge" in which male companions are allowed – whether out of politeness or irony is not certain.

In many hotels, expecially in the upper categories, the restaurants are excellent and offer first class service, so that South Africans and their guests dine far more often in hotels than we do – whether they are staying there or not.

Travelling in South Africa is a Pleasure

What you can expect in the way of transport facilities and accommodation in this country can be summed up in two words – a pleasure.

The level of development in tourism and transportation everywhere is well up to European standards, and South Africa can claim to possess the most comprehensive rail and road networks in Africa – and all in excellent condition.

By car you can get practically anywhere where there is something interesting to see. In 1983 there were 150,000 miles of road, of which 50,000 miles were tarred. This included 10,000 miles of National Highways – multi-lane carriage-ways linking the eight most important points in the country. There are 100,000 miles of untarred roads, but most of these are passable too, even after heavy rain.

In any case you can drive comfortably along the important tourist routes on well-surfaced roads, although the speed limits are different to those in Britain. Outside built-up areas – including the National Highways and despite having motorway character – the limit is 100 kph (62 mph) and 60 kph (37.5 mph) in built-up areas (unless otherwise indicated). When planning routes and schedules an average speed of 70 kph (45 mph) ought to be taken as

the upper limit, and since you want to travel and not race – the South African police keep a watchful, radar-supported eye open and fines for speeding can be heavy – you should calculate an average of about 35 mph. Journeys like Johannesburg to Cape Town – 875 miles – or Port Elizabeth to Durban – 600 miles with plenty of slow sectors winding through the mountains – add up to quite considerable times. The South Africans drive on the left side of the road.

As it is possible to rent cars on a one-way basis cheaply even for as little as three days, it is a good idea to take the train or plane for impracticable journeys and to rent a new car on arrival.

The frontiers between South Africa and the former Homelands, now regarded by South Africa as sovereign states, do not normally present any problems to car-users. Only the Transkei demands a visa, and this can be obtained at the Transkei offices in all main cities or at the border. The regulations regarding entry into the Homelands depend on the country the visitor originates from and which of the Homelands he wants to visit. Contact your Embassy or Consulate for current regulations. (See "Useful Information" on the holiday map for further details about entering South Africa.)

The railways offer a closely-knit network that reaches every notable commune and comprises 22,000 miles of track – 9,000 miles electrified.

The long distance trains in particular will enable you to cover considerable distances comfortably. All are equipped with sleeping cars included in the price of the ticket. There are only two classes: the First Class offers compartments for two or four travellers, the Second Class for three or six. Most long distance trains are furnished with a restaurant car.

Of the **express trains**, the Blue Train is probably the best known and the most luxurious. It plies between Pretoria and Cape Town and embodies every refinement imaginable from air-conditioning and showers, lounge with bar, right up to a five-star restaurant on wheels that is famous for both its culinary achievements and its service.

Another equally luxurious train is the Drakensberg Express from Johannesburg to Durban. This is not to be wondered at since prior to 1972 it covered the route Pretoria–Cape Town as the Blue Train. Train enthusiasts consider it more nostalgic and attractive than the present Blue Train – perhaps a good tip, if you fail to get a reservation on the heavily-booked Blue Train, yet would still like to experience a piece of South African railway history.

Three other expresses enrich the time-table of the South African railways: the Orange Express between Cape Town and Durban via Kimberley and Bloemfontein, the Trans-Natal Night Express from Durban and Johannesburg, and, finally, the Trans-Karoo Express plying between Cape Town and Johannesburg.

A coach service has been set up by the railways to transport passengers to the train stations, but there are also regular bus services. Luxury coaches follow a regular timetable on the various tourist routes, eg, on the Garden Route between Cape Town and Durban, or from Johannesburg to Durban through the Kruger National Park and the Hluhluwe Game Reserve.

45 minutes to 3 hours in **the aeroplane** will get you to any of the nine inland destinations of South African Airways – Bloemfontein, Durban, East London, George, Johannesburg, Cape Town, Kimberley, Port Elizabeth and Upington, plus Windhoek and Keetmanshoop in Namibia. If you intend flying a lot in South Africa, then the cheap rate VIRSA Pass for visiting foreigners is to be recommended. Enquire at your local travel agency.

Moreover, there are private airlines that fly to destinations not covered by SAA, the best known of which is probably COMAIR, short for Commercial Airways, that principally serves the airports at Kruger National Park – Skukuza and Phaloborwa. COMAIR also flies to several private game reserves in the vicinity of the Park. Further information is available from your travel agent or SATOUR.

A mobile home provides the most relaxing, independent way of journeying through South Africa. The weather conditions and roads are ideal for this type of travelling, and most of the more than 650 caravan sites are clean and well equipped. If the nearest caravan site is too far away, or if you want a change, private landowners, particularly farmers, will always allow travellers to stay one night on their grounds.

A Roof over your Head

The range of accommodation is enormous, and you will rarely be disappointed. Naturally there are differences in the quality, as everywhere else, and in South Africa that depends not only on the category – in the case of hotels – and, therefore, on the price, but on the locality, too. A first-class hotel in Johannesburg is more pretentious than a rest camp in a game reserve.

There is no risk with any **hotel** sporting the plaque showing that it is registered and regularly checked by the national hotel board. This plaque has the words „Hotelraad" at the top and the English equivalent, "Hotel Board", at the bottom, denotes the category with one to five stars and provides additional information: for example, a "T" indicates that more than half the guests are tourists, while "R" means that more than half are residents. Last not least, the type of alcohol licence is also shown. (For more about this read the chapter entitled "Palatable Pleasures" on page 82.)

Motels are to be found along the important tourist routes and exit roads from the cities. They usually have a swimming pool as well as facilities for children and are also supervised by the Hotel Board.

Rest camps inside the national parks and game reserves are remarkable for a certain primitive simplicity. The round reed-thatched huts or cottages normally have a bath or shower and some are equipped with a small kitchen. The private game reserves outside the Kruger National Park offer more comfort, indeed, luxury.

More about these in Part I – "Private Game Reserves – the Animal Kingdom on Foot".

Hiking in South Africa

The multifarious beauty of the South African countryside tempts one to want to see it on foot. This is made easier by a network of hiking paths maintained by the National Hiking Board. A whole series of delightful trails can be chosen from, in particular in Transvaal, Natal and the southern part of Cape Province. The aim is to increase the number of trails to 27, thereby completing a continuous meshwork from Soutpansberg in the north of Transvaal to the Cedarberg Nature Reserve in the west of Cape Province.

The routes are between 12 and 90 miles in length and take up to 8 days. One can spend the night in simple huts that are furnished with beds or mattresses, but one must bring one's own food and sleeping-bag.

Here is a small selection of the more rewarding trails:

– Fanie Botha Trail, in east Transvaal, starts near the Bridal Veil Waterfalls in the district of Sabie, winds through pine forests and jungle, occasionally broken up by patches of grassland, up to the summit of the 7,500 foot high Mount Anderson, the second highest elevation in Transvaal, that presents a magnificent view across the Low Veld. When this trail comes to an end at God's Window, the **Blyderivierspoort Trail** takes over, leading through the nature reserve of the same name and following the Blyde River Canyon. The hiker is rewarded by the sight of the unusual rock formations and the splendid variety of plants and animals to be found in the gorge.

– The Soutpansberg Trail in east Transvaal lies to the north of the hiking paths already described. This trail begins on the south slope of the most northerly chain of mountains in South Africa and passes through the home of the Venda nation. It is fascinating to see how the flora und fauna change on the way north over the mountains.

– Otter Trail/Tsitsikamma Coast in the easterly Cape. This trail hugs the shoreline between the Storms and Groots rivers, leading along picturesque bays, round estuaries and through dense patches of jungle. Interested observers will notice sea and river-birds as well as all kinds of marine life.

– Outeniqua Trail in the eastern Cape runs Parallel to the sea shore along a mountain saddle. Eight days are needed to complete its 80 mile trail – a part of which is the "Elephant Walk" mentioned below. Leaving the town of George the trail passes through changing countryside, past meadows filled with the national flower – protea –, through the thick Stinkwood and Yellowwood forests where the ruins of onetime golddigger camps can occasionally be seen. The wonderful scenery is brought to life by colourful birds, bushbucks, lynxes, baboons and the shy Knysna elephant.

SATOUR – the South African Tourist Office – has issued a brochure listing the current trails and the places to obtain information and make bookings.

If you prefer one-day hikes to the longer tours, then you can use the "walks". Here, too, a selection: –

– the Elephant Walk through the Knysna forest along the Garden Route.

– the Bushbuck Walk near Port Elizabeth in the east part of the Cape.

– the Lourie and the Forest Falls Walks in easterly Transvaal.

Blyde River – "The Panorama Route"

This tour is by way of being the scenic contrast to the Garden Route, though not nearly as well-known. Those who love the beauty of unusual landscapes may find this rather unfair, for the "Panorama Route" lines up a string of natural scenes that are hard to equal anywhere in the world. If you can spare a day when travelling from the Kruger National Park to Pretoria or Johannesburg, then you should arrange to take it in. One day is quite adequate, for the 45 mile trip round the Panorama Route is well sign-posted.

A substantial part of the route goes along the extreme east edge of the High Veld that constitutes 40% of South Africa. At this point the High Veld drops from a height of about 3,500 feet over a precipice to the Low Veld, some 2,000 or 2,500 feet below. Brooks and rivers have forced their way over this Great Escarpment for millions of years, carving a fantastic landscape of valleys, gorges, waterfalls and rock formations with the wierdest shapes. One of the most inventive

"pattern-makers" was the Blyde River whose handiwork can be admired along the Panorama Route, both inside and outside the **Blyderevierspoort Nature Reserve.**

A few miles after setting off in a northerly direction from **Graskop** you reach "The Pinnacle", a block of granite that protrudes high above the edge of the plateau, and get your first tremendous thrill – at "God's Window", also called "Paradise View". From a height of over 6,000 feet you have an overwhelming view into the east of the Low Veld, over the Kruger National Park as far as Mozambique, in the west of the forest-covered mountains and in the north through the Blyde River Canyon. Incidentally, God's Window is the juncture of the Fanie Botha and the Blyderevierspoort Trails that were described on page 89. If you feel like a bathe there is a path near the fork leading to God's Window that takes you to the Blyde River Pools.

A couple of miles further north a side path leads off the Panorama

Route to two waterfalls – the Berlin Falls that plunge 250 feet into a deep pond and the Lisbon Falls where the water first gathers in a pool before thundering 300 feet in a downward semi-circle.

Passing through a section of dense forests you arrive at "Bourke's Luck Potholes", surely one of the most curious natural phenomena you have ever witnessed. Sand and pebbles carried along by the water have ground deep cylindrical holes in the river-bed. From the paths and foot-bridges you can wonder at these strange shapes. As a matter of interest, the Potholes owe their name to a certain Tom Bourke who had the good fortune to discover gold at the confluence of the Blyde and Treur rivers.

From this point the Blyde River tumples fiercely into the deep Blyde River Canyon. At different points along the upper ridge you can enjoy new, breath-taking glimpses of the

2,500 ft deep gorge and the mountains peaks towering above – the Three Rondaveels and the flat-topped Mariepskop with a height of 6,375 ft.

The Panorama Route continues southwards following the road to **Vaalhoek,** which branches off at Bourke's Luck Potholes and leads along the west side of the upper Blyde River valley to **Pilgrim's Rest.** Have a look around this friendly little town that has been restored as an affectionate reminder of the days of the gold-rush and declared an historical monument. Afterwards you can return to Graskop by way of the watershed.

If you still have a little time, or can plan your journey accordingly, then drive along the section from Graskop to Lydenburg via Sabie. This will give you the opportunity to see three more splendid waterfalls: Mac-Mac, Bridal Veil and Lone Creek Falls. *(see map on page 138)*

Sun City – the Glittering Oasis.

When it is a question of spectacular shows, gaming and similarly sublime joys of life, South Africa is an absolutely parched landscape in which nothing of consequence can flourish – on account of the laws.

Neighbouring states like Botswana and Swaziland have long since taken advantage of this shortcoming and it is quite usual for cars with South African registration to be seen in the car parks of such fun-cities as Gaborone or Mbabane. But

their remote location prevents them from making a killing.

That is the object of Sun City. The citizens of Bophuthatswana had the right idea. When their patchwork state, consisting of six widely-spread Tswana regions, was granted independence in December 1977, they quickly repealed all obstructive legislation and gave the go-ahead for a show and gaming paradise, Sun City. Actually, the name belies the town for it is more a sober complex of hotels in a rocky wilderness with expensively turfed lawns and an artificial lake with a diameter of about 1,000 yards used for a wide choice of water sports. Compared to the lake the swimming pool the size of a football field looks quite modest, but is given an air of tropical romance by the palm island in the centre.

These facilities prove that Sun City is trying hard to make the day as pleasant as possible for its visitors, who have really come for the nocturnal activities. An 18-hole golf course, tennis centre and bowling arcade serve the same purpose.

But in Sun City the sun comes out at night. Illuminated by myriads of coloured lights, the hour of the shows, games of chance and good food begins. In the "Entertainment Centre" everything to do with pleasure and entertainment is effectively displayed with a technical competence that would fill Las Vegas with envy. All the more as top stars from the capital of American glamour line up behind the microphone – stars such as Frank Sinatra and Liza Minelli, to name just the most prominent. The 80-yard wide stage is the biggest in the southern hemisphere and what is presented on it is regarded by jet-setters as the best in the world.

The regular visitors to Sun City – mostly South Africans of all shades, for there is no colour bar here – really come for the gambling. Roulette, black jack, baccara, crap and everything else that the gambler's heart desires is less than a two-hour drive or a 30-minute flight from Johannesburg. 700 one-arm bandits rattle away for the casual visitor – tourists or weekend guests – who hope to get in the big-time by hitting a lucrative jackpot. Lucky winners can actually pocket up to 10,000 or 20,000 rand or more for a stake as low as perhaps six rand.

Situated as it is in Africa, Sun City would not be perfect without a typical piece of Africana. In the back garden, in a manner of speaking, lies the Pilanesberg National Park with a surface area of 230 square miles and plenty of both small and big game, in particular large numbers of the rare rhinoceros. A speciality of Sun City is hunting from open Land Rovers – something else Las Vegas cannot offer...

Sport – more a Way of Life

Hardly anything enthuses a South African more than sport – and not only as a spectator. While passions in other countries are divided amongst several different sports, in South Africa everything is concentrated on rugby, and the Republic has always been able to line up a strong national team; along with the "wallabies" and the "All Blacks", the "springboks" are doubtless one of the best known names in the game, unfortunately, not only for their sporting achievements, but also for the controversy that surrounds the team at the political level.

Rugby is also the most played sport, closely followed by soccer, tennis and golf. Fortunately, there are plenty of tennis clubs and public courts – in addition to those at the hotels – where one can play as a guest. The same applies to golf. South Africa boasts over 400 golf clubs, whose links can be used for the usual greens fee by visitors. Naturally enough, it is easier to get a game during the week. Riding and shooting are extremely popular too, and even baseball and basketball have their enthusiasts. Despite the attractive footpaths described in the chapter "Hiking in South Africa", walking is only just beginning to catch on.

Flying in all variations enjoys a certain amount of popularity in South Africa; not only engine-driven planes and gliders, but also hang-gliders and hot-air balloons. Tours for this unusual sport are offered from Johannesburg and include the flight to the Magaliesburg Mountains in the Witwatersrand.

Last but not least, the long coastline is an almost inexhaustible source for all kinds of aqua sports, primarily fishing, surfing and sailing either in yachts or catamarans. Waterskiing and aqua-diving are not so widespread, as the natural conditions are not wholly suitable. In addition, a great number of reservoirs have been turned into sports centres and are much frequented by watersport fans.

One of the nicest things about sport in South Africa is that it costs almost nothing. Annual membership fees in the majority of golf clubs, for example, are not more than R 36. If you want to have a game of tennis or golf whilst on holiday, you will not be expected to pay anything like the prices demanded in many of the traditional sun-spots.

One more thing about sport in South Africa – it is played passionately, but not taken too earnestly, one is left with the feeling that the spirit of "fair play" still has some meaning in the country.

P.S.: If you would like to have addresses of fellow enthusiasts for your own particular sport, contact the local branch of SATOUR.

Life on the Beach

Poetically, it could be said that two oceans embrace South Africa. On the west coast the Atlantic breakers bring the Benguela Current – a cool fresh body of water originating in the Antarctic – and this embrace is somewhat rough and stormy. The Indian Ocean brings the more agreeable Mozambique Current that caresses the shore gently with wind and water, but also with occasional bursts of temperament that delight the surfers.

Less poetically and more geographically expressed, South Africa has a coastal outline of 1,846 miles. Even taking the rocks and cliffs that sometimes stretch for hundreds of miles – as in Transkei – and are unsuitable for bathing into account, still leaves beaches the length and quality of which make them the envy of the classical bathing resorts in other countries.

In the first place it is obviously the South Africans themselves who make the most of these magnificent beaches, particularly in the school holidays. Just a word of warning; the summer holidays start at the beginning of December and last till the middle of January and during this period accommodation is very limited in all the local resorts. The same applies all along the Natal coast during the winter holidays which take place in June and July. If you are travelling privately and want to spend a few days on the coast at this time, then you would be well advised to book in advance. Better still if you can book your sea-side hotel through one of the internationally renowned travel agencies with branches in South Africa before leaving.

The north and south coasts of Natal are amongst the most popular in South Africa for all-year round bathing. The line between north and south is drawn at Durban and is of significance in as much as the 60-mile long and 30-mile wide coastal strip in the north from the Tugela river – the traditional border separating Natal and Zululand – to Durban is "sugar cane country" and presents fewer opportunities for bathing. On the other hand, the southerly section of the coastline from Durban to the frontier with Transkei at Port Edward is intensively exploited for the holiday trade. This section is narrower and covered with forests and pronounced subtropical vegetation. Moreover, as the mountains are nearer the coast, it rains more.

Numerous rivers flow into the sea on both coasts and form calm lagoons in the estuaries where, depending on the tributary and the tide, one can bathe very agreeably. The beaches are normally wide and shelve gradually before reaching the deeper water. At this point there is often very strong surf (much appreciated by the surf-anglers), but it is also the boundary of the swimming area, and is marked with coloured buoys, strung with strong nets to keep inquisitive sharks away.

The biggest, liveliest and most entertaining resort of the entire coast is Durban. But, in addition, you do have a choice of many resorts, large or small, elegant or simple, where the beaches are only crowded near the hotels and empty a few hundred yards further away.

But even on the picturesque Kaffraria coast between the Kei estuary (the eastern frontier to Transkei) and Port Elizabeth in the east of Cape Province the beaches are not overcrowded. This is where the transition from the summer rain region of the Natal coast to the winter rain region of western Cape Province begins (read "Climate, Weather, Travel Times"). In this zone – which continues down to Mossel Bay as the southern Cape coastline – beautiful long wide sandy beaches rise out of the sea and are lapped by long waves that can be gentle or turbulent. Large sectors of this coast run straight for miles on end – as at Wilderness –, but there are also wide bays, two of which are especially attractive: St. Francis Bay is a mecca for mussel collectors and for surf-riders who consider the 15-foot high waves that carry over half a mile second only to Hawaii; and Plettenberg Bay, famed for its three long beaches, a lagoon and a hotel constructed on the site of a former whaling station on the sea-front (Beacon Island).

Western Cape Province teems with bathing resorts on both sides of the Peninsula. On the east side, outriders of the Mozambique Current sweep warm water into False Bay, so that during the summer season from October to March the long light sand beaches of Muizenberg, Fish Hoek, Seaforth or Millers Point are alive with an exuberant variety of watersport enthusiasts. A few miles to the west, on the Atlantic, the picture is much the same, but only the hardiest go in the water. At such renowned resorts as Hout Bay, Camps Bay, Clifton and Sea Point the antarctic Benguela Current scarcely lets the water temperature rise above 15°C (60°F) even during the summer. For the same reason the coastal region north of Cape Town with such well-known resorts as Milnerton and Bloubergstrand is more for beach-lovers than swimmers.

South Africa's Animal World

South Africa can consider itself fortunate to possess such an extraordinary selection and quantity of animals. According to the statistics they are the main attraction of the country. Every other visitor to South Africa claims to have come – or to have returned – because of the animals. And even those who returned several times are not disappointed.

Sceptics – in particular those who know the big game areas of east Africa – often ask why the southern tip of the giant continent should have such an especially large variety and number of animals. One credible explanation is that during their migration from other parts of Africa the animals wandered into a kind of cul-de-sac in the south and did not attempt to get out again because the living conditions were so favourable. The richness of minerals as different as coal and gold in South Africa applies to the earth itself, offering nourishment for an extraordinary multitude of plants which in turn provide food for a variety of herbivorous animals. The climatic and geographical conditions also contributed to the development of a copious animal kingdom.

Conversely, severe interference with the animals and their living

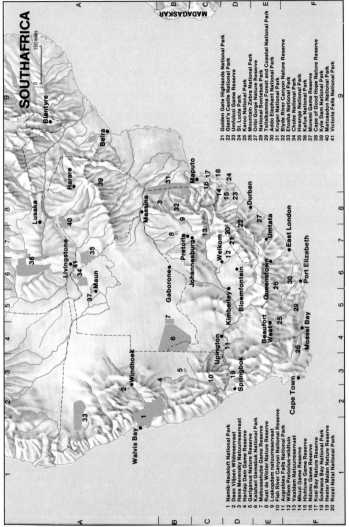

SOUTHAFRICA

MADAGASKAR

150 miles

1 Namib-Naukluft National Park
2 Daan Viljoen Wildreservaat
3 Hans Merensky Natuurreservaat
4 Hardap Dam Game Reserve
5 Gemsbok National Park
6 Kalahari Gemsbok National Park
7 Mabuasehube Game Reserve
8 Rust de Winter Nature Reserve
9 Loskopdam natuurreservaat
10 Fish River Canyon National Reserve
11 Augrabies Falls National Park
12 Willem Pretorius-wildtuin
13 Vaaldam Natuurreservaat
14 Mkuzi Game Reserve
15 Hluhluwe Game Reserve
16 Ndumu Game Reserve
17 Kosi Bay Nature Reserve
18 Sodwana Bay National Park
19 Kaffer Malsatco Nature Reserve
20 Royal Natal National Park
21 Golden Gate Highlands National Park
22 Giant's Castle National Park
23 Umfolozi Game Reserve
24 St. Lucia Park
25 Karoo National Park
26 Mountain Zebra National Park
27 Oribi Gorge Nature Reserve
28 National Bontebok Park
29 Tsitsikamma Forest and Coastal National Park
30 Addo Elephant National Park
31 Kruger National Park
32 Blyde River Canyon Nature Reserve
33 Etosha National Park
34 Chobe National Park
35 Hwange National Park
36 Kafue National Park
37 Moremi Game Reserve
38 Cape of Good Hope Nature Reserve
39 Kyle Dam National Park
40 Matusadona National Park
41 Victoria Falls National Park

96

areas could hardly be avoided while the land was being settled.

Like other parts of Africa the south was not spared the rapacity of the big game hunters and pioneers. Over and above this, the interminable conflicts, when virtually everyone was fighting everyone else, took their bloody toll amongst the animals too.

Fortunately, there were men who opposed the senseless decimation of animals early on in the history of South Africa and took the first practical steps towards the conservation of nature. For instance, Jan van Riebeeck laid down regulations to limit hunting in 1656 – just four years after the founding of the Cape Colony. However, not even more stringent regulations over a more extensive area could prevent the fact that, only 50 years later, giraffes no longer lived in the Cape and that ivory-hunters had killed off the last elephant in that region. Only a few generations later some species – the true zebra (equus quagga quagga) and the cape lion (felis leo melanochaitus) – had been wholly exterminated.

The decisive break-through in nature conservation was instigated by the President of the then Republic of Transvaal – Paul (Oom) Kruger. Proposals he made in 1884 to establish nature reserve areas were realised in 1898 in the face of considerable opposition, and it was not until 1926 – long after his death – that South Africa's first national park was set up and named in his honour: the Kruger National Park.

Since then, nine further areas have been declared national parks, some for the conservation of specific species – like the Bontebok or Mountain Zebra National Park – which does not preclude other animals from being present in large numbers. Furthermore, additional game reserves, some well worth a visit, have been set up by provincial adminstrations, particularly in Natal. Finally, thanks to the initiative of private landowners and businessmen a whole series of private nature reserves has been set up – mainly bordering on the Kruger National Park in east Transvaal – to cater to the pampered guest with luxury accommodation in the middle of the bush.

All in all, every species to be found in Africa below the Sahara is represented in South Africa's game parks. And you have the chance to meet them all in one of the many carefully maintained reserves, be it large or small, during your journey.

Where can which animals be seen?

This question is particularly of interest to those who want to see as much of South Africa's animal kingdom as possible in a limited time. The answer is in the section giving details of the individual national parks and game reserves and in the list of animal species and descriptions. Of course, this does not provide a guarantee that these animals will be seen – after all, a little hunter's luck will be needed.

Opening times and the best periods to travel. All the national parks and game reserves listed below are open all the whole year – including the Kruger National Park for which the oft-quoted seasonal closing times were lifted some time ago. (In case you intend combining a visit to the game reserves in South Africa with a trip to the Etosha Pan in Namibia, the latter is open from the 2nd Friday in March to 31st October.)

The best time to visit the game parks is thought to be between the months of August and October. In this period between the southern winter and spring the animals stay near the water-holes and the grass is still low. This enables you to observe a large number of game and to have a clear shot for your telescopic lens. If you want to observe birds more than anything else, then summer is the best time. A visit to the Kalahari Gemsbok National Park is best made from March through October.

Kruger National Park is undisputedly the most important and the most popular national park in South Africa. The area is approximately 3,500 square miles – about twice the size of Lancashire – and measures 240 miles from north to south and 40 to 60 miles from east to west. The countryside of the subtropical Low Veld varies between 600 and 3,000 ft in elevation, with small mountains, rocky peaks and overgrown river-beds. The vegetation is very varied with clusters of acacia, sparse mopane woods, dense shrubs and open prairie. Some 1,500 miles of roads lead through the park – more in the south than the north – and about a third are tarred.

In the park there are 14 rest camps with thatched huts and bungalows, restaurants and shops. Seven gates lead into the park: the

Paul Kruger Gate near Skukuza is 300 miles from Johannesburg and can be reached by car in about 9½ hours, alternatively 275 miles and a 9 hour drive from Pretoria. Flights from Johannesburg to Skukuza or Phaloborwa, or from Durban to Skukuza take 1¼ to 1½ hours.
Game. Virtually all animals indigenous to South Africa except the bontebok, gemsbok and South Africa's national animal, the springbok. If you can – or want – only to visit one game reserve, this is the best one.

Kalahari Gemsbok National Park lies in the northern tip of Cape Province on the border to Botswana and is the second biggest of the national parks with a surface area of 3,700 square miles. This park is 200 miles from Upington and can only be reached by minor roads, so that it suffers a little from being off the beaten track. This is a pity because it is totally unlike all the other national parks and thus presents complementary types of landscape and species of game. In the wide-ranging semidesert – characterized by red sanddunes sparsely covered with grass and thorn-bushes, savannah and two long dried out river-beds – it is exceptionally easy to observe the wild animals. As already mentioned, the park is open all the year round and contains three small rest camps with huts and shops with non-perishable foodstuffs. Car and coach trips from Upington to the Twee Rivieren rest camp take 8 hours. Flights in light aircraft to Twee Rivieren and Nossob about 1½ hours.
Game. The biggest game stocks in

the country, with all animals who have their habitat in this type of environment – notably, large herds of springboks, elands, brindled gnus, smaller herds of oryx and kudus. Countless animals and birds of prey, small mammals and reptiles.

Note. A visit to the Kalahari Gemsbok Park can easily be combined with a trip to Augrabies Falls National Park, about 75 miles west of Upington (see further on).

Addo Elephant National Park. This is a special park meant to protect the last elephants in the Cape. It is situated 45 miles north of Port Elizabeth at the beginning or end – depending on your itinerary – of the Garden Route on the slope of the Suurberg mountains, and has a relatively small area of 30 square miles. For this area, however, there is a lot of game that like the surroundings of the Addo Bush – trees with a maximum height of 10 foot, bushes and creepers. There are quite a few observation mounds including a few on the dam for bird-watchers. The park is open all year and can be easily reached on a day trip from Port Elizabeth. Rest camp with huts, a restaurant and a shop.

Game. The biggest collection – about 100 – of Addo elephants, black rhinos, and various varieties of antelope, like elands, kudus, duikers and bushbucks.

Mountain Zebra National Park is another park established expressly to preserve a rare breed, for this is the home of the mountain zebra. The 25 square mile reserve lies 16 miles west of Cradock on the northern slopes of the Bankberg moun-

tains in the Great Karoo and is made doubly attractive by the rocky scenery. Though open the whole year, the nights in winter can be cold and it could even snow. Accommodation is available in a modified farmhouse and small chalets. Food store. The 180 mile drive from Port Elizabeth takes about 6 hours.

Game. Some 200 of the rare mountain zebra, herds of elands, springboks, blesboks and white-tailed gnus. Plus smaller animals of prey such as desert lynx and African wildcats.

Bontebok National Park. The third of the specialized game reserves is devoted to the conservation of the bontebok that was nearly extinct 50 years ago. Located 3 miles south of Swellendam (120 miles east of Cape Town) in the open low-bush country between the Langeberg mountains and the coast. Accessible throughout the year. No accommodation, but a caravan site. Worth a detour whilst exploring the Garden Route.

Game. In addition to the 300 bonteboks there are springboks, duikers and Cape gryboks.

Cape of Good Hope Nature Reserve fills the complete tip of Cape Peninsula and you have to pass through it on your way to the Cape of Good Hope. The Cape flora is particularly beautiful and varied and features many types of protea. No accommodation. Foot-paths. 25 miles from Cape Town.

Game. Bonteboks, elands, springboks, baboons and ostriches. Wide selection of birds.

Golden Gate Highlands National Park. Beautifully situated in the Highlands (6,200–9,000 ft) of the north-easterly Orange Free State. Owes its name to the warm golden hue brought about by the light refracting off the yellow and red striped cliffs of the Maluti mountains. Can be reached easily from Johannesburg and Durban (both 240 miles) as well as from Bloemfontein (190 miles). Two rest camps with chalets, restaurant, coffee-house and shops. **Game** includes buffaloes, zebras and such rare antelopes as the blesbok and oribi. Home of the golden and the great bearded vultures.

Willem Pretorius Game Reserve – locally sign-posted as Willem Pretorius Wildtuin – is situated on the banks of the Allemanskraal Dam and contains unusually large numbers of game, including the biggest herd of black wildebeest in Africa and several uncommon breeds of antelope as in the Golden Gate Highlands National Park. Fine variety of birdlife. Rest camp that has been enlarged as a leisure centre with sports facilities. Conveniently located on the N1 (National Highway 1) between Johannesburg and Bloemfontein, 180 and 90 miles away respectively.

The Game reserves in Natal enable you to get unusually close to the game. They are quite small – even the best known one in Zululand, Hluhluwe, is less than 10 square miles in area – and one can get close-up views of the animals from hidden observation points in the company of armed game-guards,

or even go on hikes lasting several days with them. These excursions are reminiscent of the old foot-safaris in the pioneering days and lead through regions like the Umfolozi Game Reserve which is closed to motor vehicles. Accommodation in simple huts.

The scenery at **Hluhluwe** very much resembles **Umfolozi** – a slightly hilly savannah intermingled with patches of grass and river-beds. The land around the **Mkuzi Game Reserve** is flatter and more exposed, making it favourable for observing the game, in particular from the "hiding places", Bube and Msinga. Natal's most remote game reserve is **Ndumu** on the border to Mozambique. The course of the river Usutu houses a large number of crocodiles and birds. In the **St. Lucia Game Reserve** that comprises two interconnected freshwater lakes – 50 miles and 16 miles long – hippopotamuses and waterfowl dominate the scene. All these game conservation areas are open the year round. You can overnight in rest camps or private hotels and lodges, eg in Hluhluwe. The game parks are from 160 to 290 miles distant from Durban and can be reached on mostly good roads in 4½ to 9 hours.

Game. The three reserves Hluhluwe, Umfolozi and Mkuzi are primarily devoted to the two types of rhino – the square-lipped, white rhinoceros and the black rhinoceros – and you will be able to get very close to them here. But not only rhinos are represented – buffaloes, zebras and giraffes are on view too. Umfolozi also has animals of prey like lions, leopards and jackals.

Reservations for accommodation in rest camps should be made well in advance for all **national parks** by applying to: The Chief Director National Parks Board, P.O. Box 787, Pretoria 0001, Republic of South Africa. Telephone: 012–44 11 91/8. Reservations can be made up to one year in advance. There is also a central booking office for **game reserves in Natal:**

The Reservations Officer Natal Parks, P.O. Box 662, Pietermaritzburg, 3000. Telephone: 03 31–5 15 14.

If you are going on a tour organised by a travel agency, your reservations will be made for you.

The Most Important Animals in South Africa

This summary embodies not only those animals unique to South Africa, but also the most wide-spread breeds. Where known, the numbers have been added in brackets.

African Elephant (Loxodonta africana) is the biggest mammal on the continent, growing up to 10 feet and 6–7 tons in weight. Adulthood is reached at approximately 13 years, the period of gestation lasts 22 months, and they live 65–70 years. Daily nourishment consists of 400 lbs of plants and 25 gallons of water. The tusks of the male weigh up to 220 lbs, of the female 50 lbs. Elephants live in loose family units, often joining together in herds. When they are old the bulls frequently leave the herd.

In **South Africa** they can be seen in the Kruger National Park (7,500) about 25% in the south, the rest in the north and the Addo Elephant National Park (approx. 100 mostly small with shorter tusks).

White rhinoceros (Ceratotheriumsimum) or square-lipped rhino on account of its wide square upper lip. Being herbivorous it prefers the open country and was an easy target for the hunters. Light grey, up to 6 feet tall, and weighing 3½ tons. The fore-horn measures between 60 cm (2 ft) and 120 cm (4 ft), the record being 157 cm (5'1"). The rear horn is approx. 40 cm (16") – the record 56 cm (22"). Gestation 18 months, age about 45 years. Rhi-

nos do not have very good eyesight, so that you can get quite close. But beware – they react violently to beeing disturbed.

In **South Africa** they are most numerous in the game reserves of Natal (Hluhluwe, Umfolozi, Mkuzi), the Kruger National Park (500 – reintroduced after being exterminated) and above all in the Satara region and between the Sabie and Crocodile rivers.

Black rhinoceros (Diceros bicornis) characterized by its elongated upper lip. Eats mainly leaves which it tugs off branches with its lips and stays mostly in the thicket for this reason. Dark grey. Slightly smaller and lighter than the white rhino.

In **South Africa** it can be found mostly in the game reserves of Natal along with the white rhinoceros, in Kruger National Park (about 50) mainly between Skukuza and Pretoriuskop, in the Addo Elephant National Park, where, as in the Kruger Park, they have been re-introduced.

Giraffe (Giraffa camelopardalis). Grows to 5.50 m (18 ft) and can still be seen amongst the trees. Feeds on leaves and shoots that are too high for other animals. The period of gestation is 15 months; at birth the calves weigh between 100–130 lbs, are up to 1.80 m (6 ft) long and are dropped from a height of about 2 m (6'6").

In **South Africa** they can be seen in the Kruger National Park (4,200) especially around Satara and Crocodile Bridge, in the Hluhluwe and Willem Pretorius game reserves.

Buffalo (Syncerus caffer) have powerful horns as long as 1.50 m (5 ft) They stand about 1.70 m (5'6") and weigh 1,800 lbs. They live in large herds and enjoy wallowing in water. Live to 20–25 years. Grass-eaters.

In **South Africa** there are 30,000 in the Kruger Park, plus large numbers in the Addo Elephant National Park and the Hluhluwe Game Reserves.

Zebra (Equus burchelli) and the mountain zebra (Equus zebra). The savannah zebra is 1.50 m (4 ft) tall, and weighs 450 kg (1,000 lbs). Its stripes go all round its body and to the upper portions of the legs. By comparison the mountain zebra is smaller and lighter. Its stripes do not encompass the body but are very clear on the legs. Gestation and age is the same for both – 12 months and 35 years respectively.

In **South Africa** there are 19,500 in the Kruger Park and some in the Willem Pretorius Game reserve. The mountain zebra has its own national park (200) and there are about 40 in the Karoo National Park.

Brindled gnu (Connochaetes taurinus) and the **white-tailed gnu** (Connochaetes gnou) are both sturdy antelopes between 1.20 m (4 ft) and 1.40 m (4 ft 8 ins.) tall, weigh 450–600 lbs and have upturned horns and horse-tails. Gestation 8½ months. Age up to 20 years. Live in herds, often with zebras.

In **South Africa** brindled gnus are present in the Kruger National Park (7,500) and the Kalahari Gemsbok National Park. Black wildebeest may be seen in the Mountain Zebra National Park, but the lar-

1 *Kudu* · 2 *red hartebeest* ·
3 *eland* · 4 *sable antelope* ·
5 *oryx or gemsbok* · 6 *bontebok* ·
7 *njala* · 8 *impala* · 9 *springbok* ·
10 *klipspringer* · 11 *duiker*

gest herd in Africa is in the Willem Pretorius Game Reserve.

Eland (Taurotragus oryx) is the largest of the antelopes measuring 1.80 m (6 ft) and weighing 1,800 lbs. Resembles the ox. Thick spiral-shaped horns. Lives gregariously in the savannah highland to a maximum age of 12 years.

Can be found everywhere in **South Africa,** but the biggest herds are in the Kalahari Gemsbok National Park.

Gemsbok (Oryx gazella). Ruddy-grey with black and white face markings, the gemsbok is one of the most attractive of the antelopes. 1.20 m (4 ft) at the shoulder. Weight 450 lbs. Long slender fluted horns. Lives to about 19 years.

In **South Africa** in the Kalahari Gemsbok National Park and the Mountain Zebra National Park.

Kudu (Tragelaphus strepsiceros). An elegantly built antelope with grey-brown stripes running down its back. Males have widely twisted horns about 1.80 m (6 ft) long. Over 1.60 m (5'2'') at the shoulder, weight approx. 300 kg (660 lbs), age up to 11 years.

In **South Africa** they can be found in the Kruger National Park (7,500), the Addo Elephant and the Kalahari Gemsbok national parks.

Njala (Tragelaphus angasi) has curled horns like the kudu but is smaller – maximum height 1.1 m (3'8'') – and lighter – 330 lbs. The horns are only slightly curled and reach a maximum length of 80 cm (2'8''). Prefers thick undergrowth. Lives to 8 years.

In **South Africa** the njala is in the Kruger National Park (800–

1,000) – principally along the Levebu and Shingwidzi rivers –, Hluhluwe, Umfolozi and Mkuzi game reserves.

Bontebok (Damaliscus pygargus) is an endemic antelope with an undivided white spot on the forehead, white underside and white legs. Height 1 m (3'4''), weight 220 lbs, slightly curved horns up to 40 cm (16'') long with horizontal furrows.

In **South Africa** there are 300 in the Bontebok National Park and some more in the Cape of Good Hope National Park.

Blesbok (Damaliscus albifrons) resembles the bontebok in size and weight and is often confused with it. The blesbok differs in having a divided white spot on the forehead and an even, dark-brown hide that is lighter at the legs and underside, but not white.

In **South Africa** they roam the Mountain Zebra and the Golden Gate Highlands national parks.

Bushbuck (Tragelaphus scriptus). A brown antelope the size of a goat with a white half-collar and white spots on the shanks. Horns are curved, sharp as daggers and grow to 50 cm (20'') on the males. The bushbuck prefers thick bush and reeds, making it hard to be seen.

In **South Africa** they can be seen in the Kruger and Addo Elephant national parks.

Reedbuck (Redunca arundimum). Yellowish ruddy-brown antelope with sharp rounded horns that reach 45 cm (18'') on the males. Lives in the sedge and displays the white underside of its tail when running. Height approx. 1 m (3'4''), weight up to 190 lbs.

In **South Africa** the reebok – as it is sometimes called – can be observed on the river banks of Kruger Park.

Mountain reedbuck (Redunca fulvorufula) is a little smaller and lighter than the reebok, its hide is grey in hue and its horns are shorter – up to 25 cm (10″) on males – and curve forward.

In **South Africa** they can be found in the hills near Malelane in the Kruger National Park, in Mountain Zebra, Golden Gate Highlands and the Addo Elephant national parks.

Grey deer (Pelea capreolus) is similar to the mountain reedbuck in size and shape, but has a grey hide (underside of tail is white) and straight horns that can be 30 cm (12″) long on the bucks.

In **South Africa** they are in the Bontebok and Addo Elephant national parks.

Steenbock (Raphicerus campestris) is a dainty gazelle with a brown hide, large ears, and short straight horns about 20 cm (8″) long on the males. Height at shoulder about 55–60 cm (22″–24″).

They are in all **South African** national parks, though only in limited numbers.

Klipspringer (Oreotragus oreotragus). A small powerfully-built olive-brown antelope with short sharp horns – 15 cm (6″) on males – and hooves that only touch the ground at the tip.

As its name – cliff-springer – indicates, it can be found in the rocky sections of the Kruger and Augrabie Falls national parks.

Duiker antelopes – Natal duiker (Cephalophus natalensis) russet, shoulder height 45 cm (18″).

Blue duiker (C. monticola) is blue-grey in colour and the smallest antelope in South Africa – 33 cm (13″) high.

Grey duiker (Sylvicapra grimmia) yellow-brown with long legs, but still only 60 cm (2 ft) high.

In **South Africa** these tiny antelopes can be seen at following locations: Natal duiker at the Kruger Park, the blue duiker in the Natal game reserves, grey duiker at Kruger, Kalahari and Mountain Zebra national parks.

Red hartebeest (Alcelaphus caama) is a long-legged antelope that grows to 1.40 m (4′8″) and 200 kg (440 lbs). It has a remarkably long narrow head and relatively small curved horns – up to 60 cm (2 ft). Its habitat is the sparse flatland.

Can be found in all **South African** national parks except Kruger and the game reserves in Natal.

Sable antelope (Hippotragus niger) is characterized by curved sable-shaped horns that reach up to 150 cm (5 ft) and long ears. 1.40 m (4′8″) at the shoulder, weight 550 lbs, age approx. 19 years.

In **South Africa** there are 1,700 in the Kruger National Park.

Waterbuck (Kobus ellipsiprymnus) is an antelope about the size of a stag that weighs up to 300 kg (650 lbs). Its horns curve backwards and outwards and are about 1 m (3′4″) long. White circle round hindquarters. Lives to about 12 years.

In **South Africa** there are some 3,250 around the waters areas in the Kruger National Park.

Game Culling, Game Cropping

These two expressions come from the world of wildlife conservation and ecology. Culling means selection, and cropping and has the commercial implications of harvesting. Both expressions are euphemisms for the deliberate killing of wild animals for the purpose of taking measures to correct the balance of nature, after other measures (also mostly carried out by human hand) have put it out of balance.

In the game-filled South African bush and savannah, it began as it had in other parts of the continent in the last century – astronomical quantities of big-game fell victim to the unbridled rapacity of hunters, while the cultivation of enormous stretches of land fatally reduced the animals' living space. The game reserves that had been intended as islands of salvation soon revealed a fateful development: protection caused overpopulation amongst some species, so that nature was thrown off balance and threatened to produce wildlife slums. The Kruger National Park is the best example.

Culling began there with the animals of prey in order to give their prey, the out-numbered plant-eaters, a better chance to survive. But soon the opposite happened: there were so many herbivorous animals that the animals of prey could not keep their numbers in bounds, with the result that the foragers threatened to eat away their own food stocks or, as in the case of the elephants, to trample them to destruction.

After long and careful study, it is now believed that the ecological balance in the Kruger National Park is best maintained with between

Springbok (Antidorcas marsupialis), South Africa's national animal, is a rather small gazelle that grows to 80 cm (2'8") in height and 90 lbs in weight. Brown with a white underside and dark-brown stripes running along the side of the body. Short curved horns about 45 cm (18") long. The springbok is a gregarious animal that gets its name from its habit of leaping when on the run.

It can be found all over **South Africa** except in the Kruger National Park.

Impala (Aepyceros melampus). A beautiful brown gazelle with graceful horns shaped like a lyre that reach a length of 70 cm (2'4") on the males. White stomach, black stripes on white rear shanks and fetlocks. 1 m high (3'4") with a weight of 180 lbs, the impala can leap up to 10 feet high and 30 feet long.

In **South Africa** there are enormous herds south of the Sabie River in the Kruger National Park (153,000) and in the game reserves of Natal.

Warthog (Phacochoerus aethiopicus) 70–80 cm (28"–32") at the shoulder. Shaggy hair on shoulders and neck. Warts and 40 cm (16") long tusks on side of head. Charac-

7,000 and 7,500 elephants. With no other species does over-population have such drastic consequences for plant-life, and therefore for the survival of other breeds, as with the elephant. For this reason they have been the main target of culling for some years now. 450 to 500 elephants – the number corresponds roughly to the new-births – are killed off every year: either old and, therefore, dangerous loners or whole herds, including the young.

This may sound cruel but biologically it makes sense. Elephants live in family units and the young would pine to death without leadership and social ties, if they were spared. It is not in their nature to join other herds and there are not enough zoos in the world to house all the vulnerable orphans.

With elephants, as with buffaloes – whose grazing habits present no less a danger to vegetation –, game culling also means game cropping. In this case not only for the commercially valuable ivory, but also for the meat. The best cuts appear on the menues of speciality restaurants, while the rest is made into "biltong", sausage or canned meat. This is done in a meat factory belonging to the *Kruger Park*. The carcasses are brought to the factory in refridgerator vans within an hour of being shot from helicopters and disembowelled on the spot.

Moreover, game cropping has become game farming. A large number of farmers, particularly in Namibia, have taken to rearing game, such as springboks and gemsboks, on vast ranges. The animals are then slaughtered and processed in modern abattoirs. A unique example of this type of farming can be included in your tour of the Garden Route – the ostrich farms at Oudtshoorn.

teristically its tail stands up straight when running.

In **South Africa** the warthog can be seen in the Kruger National Park (3,750), Kalahari Gemsbok National Park and in Natal's game reserves.
Lion (Panthero leo). Large member of cat family. Powerful jumper. Lives in packs of 5 to 20 animals. Hunts mainly zebras, antelopes and giraffes in teams, and can achieve bursts of speed up to 30 mph over short stretches. The lion can reach 1 m (3'4") in height, 2.5–3 m (8–10 ft) in length and 250 kg (550 lbs) in weight. Period of gestation is about 3½ months with 2 to 5 cubs per lit-

ter. Life expectation up to 20 years.

There are 1,500 in the Kruger Park and more in the Kalahari Gemsbok National Park.
Leopard (Panthera pardus). Big cat that hunts antelopes, warthogs and baboons at night. Lives mostly alone or in pairs. Gestation lasts 3 months, 2 or 3 to a litter. Hide is covered with rose-shaped spots. Height 70 cm (28"). Weight up to 75 kg (165 lbs). Lives to maximum of 21 years.

Can be observed in Kruger National Park (600–900) and Kalahari Gemsbok National Park.
Cheetah (Acinonyx jubatus) is often

taken for a leopard, but has longer rear legs and is built for speed, reaching over 60 mph when hunting. Spots are round to oblong, black lines between corner of eye and mouth. Gestation 3 months, 2 to 4 cubs, age up to 16 years. Size and weight about same as leopard, though body is slimmer and longer.

In **South Africa** the cheetah can be seen in the Kruger National (250–300) and the Kalahari Gemsbok National parks.

Spotted hyaena (Crocuta crocuta) feeds off rotting carcesses and garbage, but also hunts zebra, gnu and antelopes in packs. Shoulder height 70–80 cm (24″– 28″). Period of gestation about 3 months, litters of 2 or 3. Prefers night to day. Lives to 25 years.

In **South Africa** they live in Kruger National (2,000) and the Kalahari Gemsbok National parks.

Brown Hyaena (Hyaena brunnea) recognizable by the long brown hair and wide light collar, as well as by the dog-like shape that is a little smaller than the spotted hyaena. Searches for carrion during the night.

Best seen in Kruger and Kalahari national parks around dawn.

Jackal (Canis mesomelas) feeds on carrion, but also on small animals and birds. Light red-brown with white back. About the size of a fox. Can sprint up to 30 mph.   Present in all national parks in **South Africa.**

Hunting dog (Lycaon pictus). Looks like a dog, 75 cm (2′6″) at shoulder, black-yellow spotted hide, large round or oblong ears, bushy tail. Hunting dogs are ruthless and intelligent hunters, operating in groups of up to 30.

In Kruger and Kalahari Gemsbok national parks.

Baboon (Papio ursinus) is the most frequently found monkey in South Africa, living in groups of 20 to 100 animals with strict hierarchy. Old males can weigh as much as 45 kg (100 lbs). Live till 45 years. Caution! In the conservation areas they have become persistant to aggressive by being fed.

In **South Africa** they can be seen in the hills around the Pretoriuskop and the rivers in the Kruger National Park, in the Mountain Zebra National Park and the Cape of Good Hope Nature Reserve.

Hippopotamus (Hippopotamus amphibius) is a plant-eater who spends more time in the water than on land. Height 1.70 m (5′6″), length 4.50 m (14′6″), weight 1½ to 2 tons. Eye-teeth in lower jaw grow to about 70 cm (28″). Period of gestation 7–8 months, birth and feeding of young take place under water. Hippos live up to 45 years.

In **South Africa** they can be observed in the Kruger National Park (2,350) and the Addo Elephant National Park.

The colourful bird world in South Africa is almost as rich in variety as the mammals. 900 species have been established.

The diversity of bird-life in South Africa is fascinating too: tropical and antarctic species can be found almost side by side in the Cape. The blossom of the magnificent Cape flora has induced countless birds to make their home here and – like their "new world" colleague, the sun-

bird – feed off the nectar. The only difference is that the South African honey-birds perch comfortably on the flower and use their long beaks instead of hovering. Although in no way related, their feathers are just as colourful as the sunbird and, taken together with the exuberant colours of the protea, are a constant pleasure to watch and photograph.

And merely a few miles to the west penguins inhabit many of the innumerable islands off the west coast of the Cape. They have followed the cold fish-filled Benguela Current in their hundreds of thousands to make their home on smooth rocky islets like Dassen Island, 50 miles north of Cape Town. Gigantic colonies of sea-birds such as the cormorant and the Cape gannet nest in others.

If you are both watchful and lucky, you can see how close tropical and antarctic animals can get to

each other in the Cape of Good Hope Nature Reserve; while baboons – typical representatives of the African tropics – search for food in the bush, albatross from the Antarctic circle above.

The large number of different types of birds in the national parks and game reserves makes it difficult to even list them. In the **Kruger National Park,** for example, there are 122 species of mammal, 55 kinds of reptiles and 109 breeds of fish compared to 422 varieties of birds. These include vultures, marabous, hornbills, the long-legged secretary-bird, the steel-blue iridescent Cape Glossy starling, the lilac-breasted roller and the fish eagle. The latter bears the nickname "King of the air" and is especially prevalent in the **St.**

Lucia Game Reserve in Zululand, where birdlovers can also discover a heavenly abundance and variety of river-birds: herons, wild ducks, pelicans, grey-headed herons, cormorants, spoonbills and flamingoes. The same applies to the Ndumu Game Reserve on the border to Mozambique. Primarily a bird sanctuary and has the added attraction of accommodating many east African birds – for whom Ndumu is the most southerly point they reach.

In the **Tsitsikamma Coastal National Park,** that stretches 50 miles along the coast of the Indian Ocean in southerly Cape Province, 35 different species of sea-bird can be observed. A further 175 species are at home in the woods and marshes of this park. The neighbouring **Tsitsikamma Forest National Park** accommodates such rare birds as the bright red narina trogon and the pea-green blood-red Knysna loerie.

A special attraction of the **Golden Gate Highlands National Park** is the great bearded vulture – also known as the lammergeyer – that, with the exception of Ethiopia, is seldom found in Africa. Desert birdlife is extremely easy to watch in the **Kalahari Gemsbok National Park** where there are no less than 215 different breeds, including such birds of prey as the bateleur, martial eagle and the steppe eagle. If you see enormous heaps of straw and brushwood in the acacia and thorn-trees, they are the nests of colonies of sparrow-weavers. These artistic constructions can be up to 4 metres (13 ft) in diameter and 1.50 metres (5 ft) in thickness.

Plantlife in South Africa

The diversity of fauna in South Africa may be astonishing, but it is far outstripped by the flora. Next to the large number of varieties – with between 16,000 and 18,000 there are 8 or 9 times more than in Europe – one is struck, above all, by their uniqueness.

In the south and south-west of Cape Province there is the zone of mediterranean Cape flora (Capensis). Cape Flora differentiates so starkly from other types in South Africa that it is classified as a separate "plant kingdom". This says a great deal about the quantity: some 6,000 types of plant can be seen here, of which some 200 are endemic, ie regularly found in this locality. Of these alone 69 are variations of the protea – from a total of 82 in the whole of South Africa – that grow exclusively in the winter rain region of the Cape. Absolutely the most bountiful of the plant families is the Cape Heather with more than 100 varieties.

Going eastwards – about as far as Port Elizabeth – the region runs into a zone of permanent rainfall. The largest uninterrupted forest in South Africa – 110 miles long by 10 miles wide – has developed along the coast between George and Humansdorp. Gigantic yellowwood-trees, like the Big Tree with a height of over 36 m (118 ft), tower out of a dense rain-forest covered with lianas and woody climbers. With the exception of the hardwood forest of Tsitsikamma, South Africa's woodlands consist mainly of mopane and acacia forests (Transvaal and Zululand). Taken together these account for a mere ½ per cent of the total surface of South Africa, though large areas, in particular in the Transvaal, are being converted into eucalyptus and pine-forests and over 2.5 million acres have already been transformed.

Back to the south-east coast with its subtropical climate. The coastal region of Natal on both sides of Durban presents a vivid array of indigenous scarlet coral-trees with their scarlet blossom as well as "imported" flower species like the poinsettias, frangipani, bougainvilias and the flamboyants.

Further north, in Zululand, sugar plantations dominate the vegetation and the nature reserves contain principally acacia, thorn bushes, marula and mahogany. Towards the interior the region is joined by bushland; a landscape resembling savannah with occasional parched bushes and trees – usually acacias or baobabs (monkey-Bread) – up to the frostline at 1,400 m (3,500 ft). In between there is grass that grows high in summer and withers up in winter.

A further vegetation zone is the dry area in the west that is for the most part identical with the Karoo-Namib belt. The plants that grow here have adapted to the arid conditions: stepelias, aloes and many species of succulents (plants with juicy or fleshy tissues). There are around 3,000 types of these in the dry north and the north-west corner of Cape Province!

Although the Karoo is widely characterized by low bushes, it is transformed into an authentic blaze of blossom after the first spring rains. The same is true of Namaqualand in the north-western section of Cape Province in August and September when it becomes a veritable sea of orange-coloured daisies, dotted with white, yellow, red and purple patches of other kinds of daisies.

The final vegetation zone is the Afro-Alpine floral area in the Drakensberg mountains of Lesotho and Natal. At altitudes above 2,000 m (6,500 ft) grow protea, heather, gladiolli and orchids – the last named are especially numerous in the range of mountains that extends from the Royal National Park to Cathedral Peak by way of the Giant's Castle Game Reserve. Orchids are an important part of the Cape flora, the 500 species representing one of the gems of South Africa's collection. As with the game South Africa has done a great deal to protect its flowers by establishing nature reserves and conservation laws. For example, no plants may be picked on the Veld without permission from the provincial administrator.

Moreover, a series of botanical gardens have been set up to collect and exhibit typical flowers of each particular region. Since it will hardly be possible for you to visit all the places where the many South African flowers grow wild, here is a list of the most important botanical gardens, which together will give you a comprehensive look at plantlife in South Africa.

Kirstenbosch on the slope of Table Mountain at Cape Town is wholly devoted to flowers of the Cape and is regarded as one of the most prominent botanical gardens in the world. It contains around 4,000 species of flowers, shrubs and trees over a surface of 215 acres that reaches from the foot of Table Mountain to the lofty mountain woods at Maclear's Beacon. Kirstenbosch is the National Botanical Garden and at the same time headquarters of all botanical gardens in South Africa.

Caledon. In September the nature reserve at Caledon presents the biggest wild flower show in the country.

Stellenbosch. In its "Hortus Botanicus" Stellenbosch displays not only a representative selection of Cape flora, but also such rarities as the prehistoric welwitschia – a plant typical of the Namib desert.

Worcester is famous for its "Karoo Botanic Garden". It is the oldest offshoot of Kirstenbosch and one of five internationally recognized gardens for succulents.

Port Elizabeth. The Settler's Park Nature Reserve offers a survey of the wide spectrum of Cape flora, in particular the flowers of the eastern Cape.

Pietermaritzburg has devoted its botanical garden to the flora of Natal, but also presents a wealth of azaleas, rhododendrons, camelias and plane-trees.

Durban has one of the most complete collections of orchids in its botanical garden – a collection of world-wide significance.

Harrismith houses flowers from the Drakenberg mountains in its botanical garden. This garden is one of the highest in South Africa and has plants that grow above 1,500 m (5,000 ft).

Nelspruit displays the subtropical diversity of the Low Veld in its botanical garden.

Johannesburg has created "The Wilds": a landscape garden in which all kinds of wild flowers can be seen, though the accent is on those from the Witwatersrand.

"Whites" – "Non-whites"

This sign can still be seen over many public facilities in South Africa today. Since experience has shown that it is not difficult for both whites and non-whites to recognise foreign visitors, any faux pas will usually end up by your being shown in a friendly manner where you "belong". Still, you ought to know what is segregated (incidentally, park benches are no longer segregated, but parks are): on the railways – trains, or rather sections of trains, waiting rooms, platforms and toilets; public buses (with the exception of Cape Town which is a little more tolerant in racial questions in any case); public offices; shops, including the "bottle stores" or Off Licences which have two entrances and two sales areas immediately next to each other; hospitals and picnic sites in the national parks. Beaches are partially divided into sections for "Whites" and "Non-

whites", although this discrimination has been lifted in most parts of the Cape and it is intended to do so along the coast of Natal as well. Hotels and restaurants are normally segregated, but the "international hotels" are excluded and may be frequented by non-whites.

Local transport is primarily designed for the non-white population. For instance, the buses in Johannesburg carry mainly passengers from Soweto to the city centre an the industrial areas. The majority of cars that can be seen during the rush-hour are driven by whites and it is part of the white way of life to walk as little as possible in the towns. This is why you will hardly ever see anyone window-shopping in the evening, unless it be in a relatively enclosed precinct such as the Carlton Centre in Johannesburg.

The Population of South Africa

(1980 census)

Total population	23,771,960	
Africans	15,970,019*	
Whites	4,453,273	
Coloureds	2,554,039	
Asians	779,463	

* This figure does not include the population of the independant Homelands of Venda, Transkei and Bophuthatswana. It should, however, be reduced by the 920,000 Africans in Ciskei which was granted independence at the end of 1981.

South Africa's Neighbours

To have neighbours not only on the other side of the fence but also in one's own garden, as it were, is a constellation with which South Africa has enriched our world – a world that is not exactly devoid of peculiarities! That the fences have varying heights – in Namibia it is de facto non-existent – seems to be a triviality.

The good neighbourly relationships are above all the result of behaving well to the economic giant, South Africa, as an obvious consequence of being commercially dependent on it. This certainly applies to the former Homelands that have been granted independence – Transkei, Bophuthatswana, Venda and Ciskei – but also to a large extent to Botswana, Lesotho and Swaziland which, for example, could hardly exist without food supplies from South Africa. Even South Africa's political opponent, Mozambique, would be very reluctant to forgo the gold and foreign currency inflow from its unloved neighbour that pays 60% of the wages of the innumerable workers who commute from Mozambique in gold, and purchases a major share of the electricity produced by the Cabora Bassa Dam.

Here is an ABC of South Africa's internal and external neighbours. Namibia has been excluded, since it has a chapter to itself.

Bophuthatswana

Independent since 1977 (though only recognized by South Africa), from 1972 it had been a self-governing territory. Size: 15,550 square miles, divided into six parts in the northwest of Cape Province, in western Transvaal and in the middle of the Orange Free State. 1.2 million Tswanas inhabit South Africa and are regarded as citizens of Bophuthatswana. Cattle breeding and mining, especially platinum (largest platinum mine in the world). Currency: South Africa rand. South Africa is almost the only trading partner.

Bophuthatswana has gained a certain touristic importance through Sun City (see page 91).

Botswana
(formerly Bechuanaland)

Granted independence by Great Britain in 1966 and internationally recognized. Size: 231,000 square miles. 850,000 inhabitants mostly Sotho-Tswanas. Animal farming and mining, notably diamonds, copper, nickel. Currency: Pula. Economy is closely linked with South Africa. Member of South African Customs Union. A part of the male population works in South Africa, most in the diamond mines at Kimberley.

The country consists mainly of desert and savannah and has not been opened up much to tourism. But Botswana does own the Okawango Marshes in the north, one of the few untouched natural regions of Africa with many waterfowl, crocodiles, hippos and plenty of big game like elephants, giraffes and antelopes. Game Reserves: Chobe and Moremi Park.

Ciskei

Independent since 1981 (despite a protest by the UN, and therefore not internationally recognized, except by South Africa), previously a self-administered territory from 1972. Size: 2,000 square miles, surrounded by eastern Cape Province. 1,070,000 inhabitants predominantly Xhosas, of whom approx. 440,000 live as guest-workers in the Republic of South Africa. Agriculturally self-supporting, economically dependent on South Africa. Currency: South African rand.

Hardly opened up to tourism, widely pristine countryside – forests, mountains, coast.

Lesotho
(formerly Basutoland)

Kingdom granted independence by Great Britain in 1966. Internationally recognized. Size: 11,675 square miles. Approx. 1,370,000 inhabitants almost exclusively Sothos. About 10–15% of the population live for 12–18 months in South Africa as guest-workers. Animal products – principally wool –, diamonds. South Africa is virtually sole trading partner. Currency: Loti (Plural: Maloti), South African rand is legally recognized as means of payment. Cus-

toms Union with South Africa.

There is no intensive tourism in Lesotho yet. The Highland, that ranges from 2,000 m (6,550 ft) to 3,500 m (11,500 ft) and covers two thirds of the country's surface, offers good opportunities for active holidays, such as hiking, mountain climbing and skiing in June and July.

Mozambique

A Portuguese colony until 1975, since then a socialist-orientated People's Republic. Size: 30,745 square miles. Approx. 12.1 inhabitants 90% members of various Bantu tribes (Makua, Tonga and Shona), about 120,000 are guest-workers in the Republic of South Africa. Agricultural products, ores. Currency: Metical. Trading partners: EEC, South Africa, Portugal, USA, etc.

In spite of good beaches and a wealth of game, Mozambique has hardly had any significant tourism since 1975.

Swaziland

Kingdom made independent in 1968 by Great Britain. Internationally recognized. Size: 6,680 square miles. Bordered by Transvaal in the north, west and south, and by Natal and Mozambique in the east. 550,000 inhabitants 90% Swazi. Agricultural produce – primarily sugar, cotton, citrus fruits – iron ore, asbestos. Currency: Lilangeni (Plural: Emalangeni). Trading partners: South Africa, Great Britain, Germany. Member of South African Customs Union.

Swaziland is touristically aimed at South Africans who visit the country on account of the less stringent laws – eg gambling.

Transkei

Independent since 1976, not recognized internationally (except for South Africa). In 1963 Transkei became first of the self-administered territories. Size: 16,540 square miles. Divided into three parts bordering on Cape Province, Lesotho and Natal. Approx. 2.5 million inhabitants, predominantly Xhosa, of whom about 600,000 live in the Republic as guest-workers. Agriculturally self-supporting. Economically dependent on South Africa, the sole trading partner. Currency: South African rand. Customs and Currency Union with South Africa.

Scarcely any tourism in spite of beautiful coastline ("Wild Coast") and charming hilly country in interior with the rondaveel huts of the Xhosas who have a predilection for red and orange ("Land of the red blankets"). Most tourists only pass through on the National Highway N2 between Durban-East London.

Venda

Independent since 1979, not recognized internationally (except by South Africa), from 1969 self-administered territory. Size: 2,500 square miles situated in north-east Trans-

vaal near border to Zimbabwe. Approx. 500,000 inhabitants almost exclusively Venda. About 110,000 work in South Africa. Subtropical, agricultural products like coffee, bananas, tea, avocados, etc, but also minerals such as graphite, phosphate and magnesium. Wholly dependent on South Africa for trade. Currency: South African rand.

Despite picturesque unspoilt countryside, very little tourism.

Zimbabwe
(formerly Rhodesia)

British colony prior to being granted independence in 1980: Size: 150,240 square miles. Approx. 7.5 million inhabitants of whom 95% Africans (mostly Shona and Ndebele), 4.5% Europeans and 0.5% coloureds, of mixed blood, and Asians. Agricultural produce, especially beef, tobacco, cotton and mining products such as asbestos, chrome-ore, copper and tin (70 different minerals in total). Biggest trading partner is Great Britain followed by Zambia, South Africa, EEC countries and Japan. Currency: Zimbabwe dollar.

Along with South Africa Zimbabwe is the most popular country for tourists in this region. The three main attractions – Victoria Falls, the remnants of the old city of Zimbabwe and the Hwange (formerly Wankie) National Park – are considered highlights by many touring southern Africa, and one, if not all three, are often included in tours.
(TAR)

Namibia

and in the middle, creations of a culture thousands of years old: ravishingly beautiful rock paintings and engravings. In addition, rock formations that are so curious that it is hard to find their equal anywhere, gorges that have been cut into the hard rock by millions of years of water erosion, and flora that shows the different ways plants can adapt to dryness and heat. But Namibia was also the first German colony, and one hundred years later the German influence is still very much in evidence.

Namibia is worth more than just a 3 day trip to the Etosha Pan!

At first glance, Namibia (or South West Africa until the United Nations re-named it in 1968) does not appear to be a particularly attractive place to spend a holiday. For many visitors – especially those in a hurry – the "only" thing worth seeing is one of the biggest game reserves on earth, Etosha. (And, truly, that alone is worth a visit). But there is more. One of the most extensive deserts in the world runs parallel to the Atlantic Ocean for 875 miles; the multifarious colours and shapes of its dunes make the Namib Desert one of the great natural wonders of Africa. Sun-scorched mountains and rocks,

Country and climate

Namibia has an area of 316,600 square miles and is more than three times larger than the U.K. The interior is comprised principally of an arid mountainous plateau with an elevation of 1,000–2,000 m (3,300–6,600 ft) that falls away in the northeast and south-east into the dry low plains of the Kalahari in Botswana and the Karoo in South Africa. In the west the plateau swings down to the 50–75 mile wide coastal belt of the Namib Desert, and in the north it merges with the flat bushland to which the Etosha Pan belongs.

The climate, with hot days and cool nights, is typical of semi-desert regions. The temperature in summer can easily exceed 40 °C (104 °F), while it is moderately hot in winter. The temperature in the central highlands is a little lower than in the remainder of the interior. On summer afternoons the quicksilver usually stays below 40 °C (104 °F) and in winter hovers at an agreeable 25 °C (77 °F) in the shade; thoroughly acceptable with a humidity of between 10–30%. Along the coast the Benguela Current mitigates the heat of the Namib Desert and affects the fog that is characteristic of this region in autumn, winter and spring.

In the interior there are normally two periods of rain: a brief period sometime between October and December and a longer one between January and April. However, as the droughts of the past years have shown, this rain is not very reliable, so that artificial wells are often the last resort for the farmers. Adequate rain, mostly in the form of thunderstorms, really only occurs in the north and north-east where the Etosha Pan is located. For this reason the Pan is inaccessible from November through March.

Population and history.
The Ovambos with 1.1 million form the biggest portion of the population – about a half. Other important groups are the Damara, Nama, Herero, Bushmen and the Tswana. The whites represent 11.6%. With 3.4 inhabitants per square mile Namibia is one of the most thinly populated countries on earth. The coast of Namibia was discovered in the 15th century by Portuguese mariners. Great Britain annexed Whale Bay in 1878; in 1883 a German merchant named F. A. Lüderitz purchased what later became known as Lüderitz Bay from the Namas, and in 1884 the German government declared an extensive strip of coast a protectorate (German South West Africa). By 1893 the young colony had grown to the borders of the present Namibia. In the years 1903 to 1907 the Herero and Nama tribes revolted against German imperialism at great cost to the black population. The colony was granted limited self-government in 1909. One year after the outbreak of World War I the German troops capitulated to South Africa, thus ending German colonial control. In 1920 South Africa received a mandate over the south-west. This was retracted by the UN in 1966 who re-named it Namibia. Since then there have been considerable international differences about Namibia's status and its progress towards becoming an independent republic.

The economy
Animal breeding – including the production of caracul pelts, representing around 50% of the world production – is one of the pillars of Namibia's economy, although in terms of value the major part is taken up by mining products, principally diamonds but also uranium, copper, lead, tin and wolfram. An important branch of industry is fishing and fish products. (The figures for imports and exports are contained in those for South Africa).

Major tourist attractions
If the criterion is what attracts and interests the most visitors – especially from Europe – then the Etosha Pan in the north of Namibia undisputedly heads the list of tourist attractions.

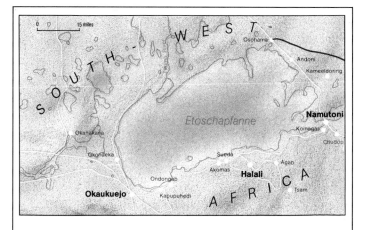

The Etosha National park, the heart of which is the Etosha Pan, has been deliberately reduced several times from its original size of 40,000 square miles in order to allow the native tribes around the park more living space, as well as to facilitate the erection of a 10 ft high 500 mile long fence, the purpose of which is to prevent the game from straying away and poachers from getting in, or at least to make it more difficult for them to get in. Even today the Etosha National Park still covers an area of 8,565 square miles, making it bigger than the Kruger National Park in South Africa.

In this game reserve, undoubtedly the most important of the subcontinent with a landscape ranging from dense bush to wide open plains, live colossal herds of animals as free and unmolested as in earlier times before civilisation made its mark.

During the dry winter months the Etosha Pan at the centre of the park attracts enormous numbers of animals. The summer rains have filled the 2,000 square mile dry lake, that was formed 70 million years ago, with water that seeps into the ground and supplies innumerable waterholes which become drinking troughs for the game in the dry period. The constant coming and going of the animals, the sight of different species living peaceably side by side, as well as the pitiless battles for status and prey fascinate time and time again.

About 40 waterholes have been set up for visitors to watch the game. Some 500 miles of rough roads link these observation points with each other and with the three rest camps Namutoni, Halali and Okaukuejo. The latter is the main camp and offers the best chance of accommodation. Nearby is a waterhole that is lit up at night so that the game can be observed after sunset.

Game. The park houses most wild animals to be found in southern Africa. Huge herds of springboks, giraffes, gnus and zebras can be seen everywhere. All sizes and breeds of the antelope family are represented, from the eland and kudu (especially in the Namutone district) to the oryx (or gemsbok) and, the smallest of all, the Damara dik-dik. Lions can be seen easily and often, while cheetahs and leopards need a bit of luck. Elephants often reside in the middle of the park but like coming to the illuminated waterhole at Okaukuejo, too. Rhinos are rarer and live above all in the west section of the park. The bird world is also well represented with 325 species from the ostrich to the heraldic bird of Namibia, the crimson-breasted shrike.

Etosha is open to visitors from the second Friday in March to the 31st October.

The Namib-Naukluft Park is not nearly as well known as or as popular as Ethosha but its natural wonders make it just as fascinating.

The 8,850 square mile park is the most extensive nature reserve in the country and was established in 1978 by consolidating the Namib Desert Park with the Naukluft Mountain Zebra Park. A splendid array of geological formations, plants, mammals and birds are now united within its boundaries. Herds of oryx, springboks and zebras wander over the grassy plains and granite rocks. Typical are the apricot coloured dunes that rise up to heights of 300 m (1,000 ft), a lagoon that is a paradise for seabirds and riverbirds alike and parched plains where unique plants that have adapted to the desert conditions thrive, like the prehistoric welwitschia mirabilis. Canyons, caves and watercourses that cleave into the dolomite rocks. All in all, a natural, once in a lifetime experience.

Further places of interest are the capital of Windhoek, the Swakopmund harbour, the Fish River Canyon and many, many more – all described in the "A to Z" starting on page 122. To make it simpler the key-words for places in Namibia have been marked with a cross (+).

Travelling in Namibia
The quickest description is to say that it is just as pleasant as in South Africa (see page 86). The network of roads between the 15 largest towns is made up of modern tarred roads. Unmade roads – "pads" in Afrikaans – need only be used if you drive off the main routes or through the nature reserves. Renting a car is advisable if you intend to seek out places off the beaten track, eg the sites of prehistoric rock artistry at Khorixa and Twyfelfontein or places of interest like Brukkaros, Kokerboom Forest and Fish River Canyon. In such a thinly populated country there is naturally enough not much traffic, so that you will have quite a few lonely stretches to cover. This also means taking some precautions which will be explained when taking possession of your hired car.

The railways are concentrated on the main line from Windhoek via

The Kaiser in South Africa

Where tourists now spend their evenings with a cool beer was once the site of military roll-calls. The guest-rooms around the pretty courtyard at the Namutoni rest camp in the northerly Etosha Game Reserve are encircled by battlements. For this is the old fort used by the Kaiser's colonial troops at the end of the last century to control access to Ovamboland.

During the course of the native rebellion 500 Ovambo warriors attacked the fort on 28th January, 1904. The troops were out on patrol and the fort was empty save for seven sick soldiers who had been left behind and who were able to slip away under cover of darkness to Tsumeb, the nearest town.

The Ovambos destroyed the fort, but it was re-built and handed over to South African troops in 1915. It gradually fell into ruin until the post-war administration came up with the idea of declaring it an historical monument and restoring it as a rest camp for visitors to the National Park. Today it stands out snow-white with its battlements against the flat savannah.

The main turret has been converted into a museum recording the history of the fort and the events of that 28th January in 1904. The flag of Kaiser Germany that flew above the fort until 1915 is also on display.

Much of the German colonial heritage in South West Africa has remained undisturbed since the end of the First World War. The bronze monument of the German cavalryman (The Reiter Memorial) still stands high above Namibia's capital city, Windhoek, and on the plinth is carved – in German and with typical Prussian accuracy – the exact number of the military and civilian victims of the Herero and Hottentot rebellion from 1903 to 1908. Still, the memorial is one of the most beautiful in the country with a rugged beauty of its own that holds every visitor spellbound.

Keetmanshoop to Upington, the junction joining up with the South African network. Side lines lead to Otjiwarongo, Outjo and Tsumeb (approx. 600 miles before the Etosha Pan) as well as to the ports of Swakopmund, Walvis Bay and Lüderitz.

Namibia's international airport at Windhoek has direct flights to Europe, to Johannesburg and Cape Town. Light aircraft are employed for internal flights between Namibia's 20 airfields.

The rest camps round the Etosha Pan offer modern accommodation with two, three or six beds, running hot and cold water, and some of the rooms are also equipped with a refridgerator and a kitchenette. However, the accommodation is more simple than luxurious.

South Africa and Namibia A to Z

(Places in Namibia = +)

Addo Elephant National Park
(F6), game reserve to protect the last elephants in the eastern Cape region. (cf p. 98).

+ **Ai-ais** (C2), holiday resort and spa with hot waters at the terminus of the Fish River Canyon. Only open from mid-March to beginning November (cf Fish River Canyon).

Apple Express (F5/6), narrow-gauge railway through orchard district of the Langkloof valley near Port Elizabeth. Special rides at weekends May-January on veteran steam engines and carriages Port Elizabeth – Loerie (cf p. 49).

Augrabies Falls National Park (C3/4), waterfalls on Orange River that plunge 145 m (475 ft) into the biggest and longest granite canyon in the world. During the high-water period (late summer, ie March) 19 falls along the canyon. Next to the Victoria Falls, the most interesting falls in Africa. Plentiful flora including "kokerboom" and other species of aloes. Many baboons and small antelopes, especially klipspringers. (Thus the Klipspringer Trail, a three-day hiking route along the canyon). Rest camp with shop and restaurant. In the north-west of Cape Province near Upington, therefore easy to combine with visit to Kalahari Gemsbok National Park (cf p. 98).

Badplaas (B8), holiday resort and spa with sulphurous waters in attractive hill country near the Swaziland border.

Barberton (B8), one of the sites of the first gold-rush (1883), with many old well-maintained buildings.

Barkly West (C5), old diamond town on Vaal River in which diamonds are still sought during the dry period (June-November). Original bridge and customs house from 1886 (Historical monument).

Beaufort West (E4), historic town founded 1820, today the largest in the Karoo. The old Town Hall (Historical monument) is now a museum with, amongst other exhibits, mementoes of Napoleon. Centre of sheep-rearing country. Only town in South Africa with pear-trees lining the streets. Nearby, Karoo National Park (cf same).

+ **Bethanien** (C2), small locality with early residence of Schmelen (Schmelenhaus), a missionary. The house was erected in 1814 and is the oldest in the country. Historical monument and museum.

Bidouw Valley (E3), remote valley in Namaqualand renowned on account of its many species of wild spring-flowers.

Bloemfontein (D7), capital of the Orange Free State and seat of South Africa's Supreme Court. Important centre of industry and administration. University. Naval Hill is a nature reserve in the middle of the city offering a good view. The Presidency dating from 1886 and the first Council Chamber (Raadsaal) from 1849. Beautiful parks.

Bloubergstrand (cf map on p. 128), small town on Table Bay on the "other side" to Cape Town with the prettiest (and most photographed) view of Table Mountain. Very good surfing and excellent restaurants.

Blyde River Canyon (B8), 10 miles long and 600 m (2,000 ft) deep in places, one of the great natural wonders of South Africa. More in special chapter on p. 90 and map on p. 138.

Boekenhoutfontein near Rustenberg (B7) was once Paul Kruger's farm. The buildings give impression of pioneer architecture between 1841 and 1892.

Bontebok National Park (F4), near Swellendam, houses the last great herds of one of the rarest antelopes, the bontebok.

+ Brandberg an isolated chain of mountains containing the highest peak in South West Africa, the 2,579 m (8,455 ft) high Königstein. Famous because of the "White Lady of Brandberg", an unusually beautiful and mysterious Bushman rock drawing in a cave in the Tsisab gorge.

+ Brukkaros (B2), extinct volcano 1,580 m (5,180 ft) high with a diameter of 2,000 m (6,550 ft). Good site for studying the sun's rays.

+ Burnt Mountain, a natural phenomenon in north-west Namibia. A mountain peak near Twyfelfontein whose lilac red rock appears dark crimson in the light of the setting sun. The vertically eroded basalt rock face on a nearby mountain slope looks like organ pipes.

Caledon (F3), renowned for its mineral water springs and the 25 acre botanical garden with many species of wild flowers and aloes (Flower show at blossom time in September, October).

Cango Caves (F4), near Oudtshoorn, 800 m (880 yds) of caves with bizarre stalagmites and stalactites. The Grand Hall, 16 m (52 ft) high and 107 m (350 ft) wide, is the biggest of 80 chambers. The largest stalactite towers 12.5 m (41 ft). The Grand Hall is one of the most interesting caves in the world.

Cape Agulhas (F3), geographically the southern-most point of Africa. Lighthouse from 1849.

+ Cape Cross, north of Henties Bay (A1), marks the spot where the Portuguese mariner Diego Cao first put foot on south-west African soil in 1485. Today tens of thousands of seals live here in the Cape Cross Seal Reserve. Open daily from beginning of December till end of February, at Easter and every weekend thereafter until end of June.

Cape of Good Hope (F3), the southern tip of Cape Peninsula where the Atlantic and Indian Ocean meet. The lighthouse at 244 m (880 ft) altitude offers good view of the Cape of Good Hope and False Bay (cf same and map opposite).

Cape of Good Hope Nature Reserve (F3 and map on p. 96), established to protect the flowers and animals of the Cape Peninsula (cf. p. 96).

Cape Town (F3), South Africa's "mother city" founded in 1652 as a victualling station for the Dutch East India Company. Picturesque position between Table Mountain and Table Bay makes it one of world's loveliest cities. Capital of Cape Province. Seat of South African Parliament. Approx. 1.5 million inhabitants, mostly coloureds. Oldest historic building is the Castle of Good Hope dating from 1666 with its Military and Marine Museum and the Fehr Collection of antique furniture and glassware,

Chinese pottery and paintings depicting South African history. Other parts of this collection are to be found in the old residence "Rust-en-Vreugde" that dates from 1777. The Koopmans de Wet House with its vast collection of furniture and other antiques gives a good insight into the 18th century living style of the upper class. Further attractions: the Groote Kerk (the oldest church in the city), Company's Garden (once the fruit and vegetable garden of the victualling station), the Malay Quarter (the oldest in the city), Parliament buildings, the university. Adderley Street is the main shopping street and most of the attractions are within walking distance. More about Cape Town in the chapter: "The mother city and her fair Cape".

Cedarberg (E3), a rugged mountain wilderness in the west of Cape Province. Unusual rock formations and rock paintings as well as diverse flora.

Ceres (F3), picturesquely situated in the Dwars River Valley and surrounded by mountains, Ceres is often called the Switzerland of South

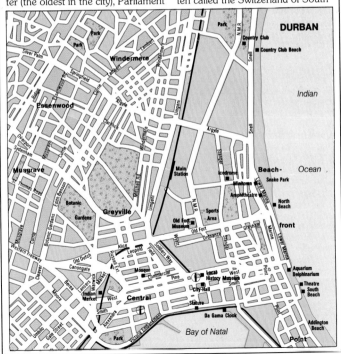

Africa. One of the main apple-growing regions.

Citrusdal (E3), one of the foremost orange-growing areas. At the foot of the Cedarberg mountain.

Clanwilliam (E3), located in a warm fertile valley where "rooi"-tea, subtropical fruit and tobacco grow. A short distance outside the town is the Ramskop Wild Flower Nature Reseve (blossom-time between July and mid-September, depending on rainfall).

Cradock (E6), in the upper valley of the Great Fish River. Sheep-breeding, fruit-growing. Dutch Reformed Church built in 1867 is a copy of London's St. Martins-in-the-Field. The van Riebeeck Karoo Garden with different types of succulents. Egg Rock, an enormous egg-shaped pinnacle. Nearby the Mountain Zebra National Park.

Cullinan (B7), the first diamond mine near Pretoria where the world's largest diamond – the 3,106 carat Cullinan Diamond – was found in 1905. It was broken down into 9 large and 96 smaller stones, amongst them the 530 carat Star of Africa which is set in the British sceptre. The mine can be viewed.

+ **Daan-Viljoenwildreservaat** (A2), about 15 miles west of Namibia's capital, Windhoek, in the Khomas Highland. This game reserve has a diversity of game, such as gemsboks, kudus, mountain zebras, springboks and gnus but no animals of prey, so that it possible to hike. Rest camps with bungalows, a restaurant, caravan park and swimming pool. Popular holiday resort.

De Wildt (B7), about 15 miles west of Pretoria, research and breeding station for cheetahs and other rare animals. Can be visited.

Durban (D8), with almost a million inhabitants South Africa's third largest city and most important harbour. Biggest portion of the population are Indians brought to the country after 1860 to work on the sugar plantations. Oldest Hindu temple in South Africa in the Umgeni Road. Indian market with many different exotic goods. Oriental bazaar near the magnificent moslem mosque in Grey Street. Main shopping street is West Street where the Town Hall with the Durban Museum is located (impressive collection of South African birds including the only preserved skeleton of the extinct Mauritius dodo). Historically interesting: the Old Fort and the Old House Museum, a 19th century colonial house with authentic furniture. Botanical garden with famous orchid house (3,000 sorts from all over the world). Sugar Terminal in the harbour is worth seeing. Beach front with the "Golden Mile" (a promenade with amusement parks), aquarium with dolphin shows, snake park with most breeds of South African snakes where serum is collected, bowling, swimming baths and naturally the colourful rickshaw-boys with their spangled headwear. On both sides of Durban are resorts such as Umhlanga Rocks, very popular with Europeans.

+ **Duwisip** (B2), historic castle on edge of Namib Desert with interesting collection of furniture and weapons from the 17th and 18th century.

East London (F7), only port in South Africa located on a river (the estuary of Buffalo River) and one of the major ports for Orange Free State. Gateway to Ciskei and Transkei. Three beaches in city itself and several others outside. Museum comprising one of the most comprehensive natural history collections in the country including the world famous coleacanth, a primeval fish with leg-like fins believed extinct for 50 million years and caught near East London in 1938. Moreover, probably the only egg of the Mauritius dodo in existence. Extensive collection of South African mussels.

Echo Caves (B8), 16 caves with dolomite-stone stalactites about 200 m (660 ft) deep. Once refuge for African tribes. Museum of Man exhibiting finds from the Stone Age.

Eland River Falls (B8), 90 m (300 ft) waterfall where the Great Escarpment drops from the Transvaal Highland to the Lowland. Nearby is the 400 m (440 yds) long tunnel, now shut down, of the NZASM railway line to Mozambique constructed in 1892–93.

+ **Etosha National Park,** one of the best-known and largest game reserves in the world in the north of Namibia contains the Etosha Pan, a 2,000 square mile dry lake (cf p. 119 and special map).

False Bay (F3), wide sweeping bay on the east side of the Cape Peninsula with long beaches and such popular resorts as Fish Hoek, Kalk Bay, St. James and Muizenberg. "Historical mile" from Simonstown, main port of the South African navy (cf special map on p. 128).

+ **Fish River Canyon** (C2), one of the great natural wonders of Africa in the south of Namibia near the border with South Africa. A 100 mile long canyon carved 550 m (1,800 ft) deep and 27 m (90 ft) wide by the Fish River. A mighty primordial landscape as impressive as the Grand Canyon in the USA. Apart from late summer (around March) the river is dry and its sandy pebbled bed only interspersed with occasional pools. On the east side of the canyon there is a 40 mile long road leading to numerous observation points. A 55 mile hiking trail begins at Ai-Ais (cf same). The 4-day hike through the river-bed is strenuous and has to be authorized (only beginning May to end August).

Franschhoek (F3), small wine community in wide Berg River Valley founded in 1688 by Huguenots. Huguenot memorial and museum. Lovely historic Cape Dutch estates once belonging to French settlers like La Motte, Cabrière, La Dauphine, etc in the vicinity.

Garden Route (F4/5/6), South Africa's dream road along Indian Ocean between Mossel Bay and Storms River.

George (F4), ancient town founded in 1812 at foot of Outeniqua mountains. Smallest Anglican cathedral in the world, St. Mark's. One of the most popular resorts along the Garden Route with several sandy beaches. Centre for aquatic sports.

Genadendal (F3), first mission in South Africa dating from 1737. Beautiful old houses and oak groves; watermill and church clock from early 18th century.

Giant's Castle Game Reserve (D8), mountain park in the Drakensberg mountains on the border separating Natal and Lesotho. Large variety of wild flowers and game.

Good opportunities for mountain climbing and hiking. Prehistoric rock paintings.

Golden Gate Highland National Park (C/D7), park in north-east Orange Free State renowned for its beautiful scenery.

Graaff-Reinet (E5), one of the oldest and most remarkable little towns in South Africa, founded in 1786, classical examples of Cape architecture. Reinet House built in the settler period, now museum with valuable furniture, weapons and coaches. In the courtyard is the biggest vine in the world; planted in 1870 its "trunk" has a circumference of 2.30 m (7′6″) and a height of 1.50 m (5 ft). Dutch Reformed Mission church dating from 1821 carefully restored, as is the thoroughfare Stretch's Court.

Grahamstown (F6), lovely old town with probably the best maintained houses from the late Georgian period. Two cathedrals, Rhodes University, botanical garden and Albany Museum with the largest herbarium in South Africa.

Graskop (B8), little town in the Dra-

JOHANNESBURG

kensberg mountains in Transvaal serving as point of departure for the Panorama Route along the Blyde River Canyon (cf p. 138 and special map).

Griquatown (D5), missionary town from 1800s. Tiger's-eye and other semi-precious stones are found round about and can be purchased from cutters in the town.

Groot Constantia (special map on p. 138), residence of Simon van der Steel, the Governor under whose supervision this famous example of Cape Dutch architecture was built. The ornamental gable of the wine-cellar, now a wine museum, is of exceptional beauty. The manor house is also a museum containing a lovely collection of furniture, paintings and china.

+ **Grootfontein,** charming little town in northern Namibia, centre of important livestock region. The biggest meteorite in the world, weighing 50 tons and 82% of iron, is in the grounds of Hoba farm in the vicinity.

Harrismith (C7), in eastern Orange Free State west of the Drakensberg mountains. Health resort. Famous for the 150 million old petrified tree near the Town Hall and the Bushmen paintings nearby.

Heidelberg (B7), south-east of Pretoria, has an interesting transport museum in the old railway station built in 1895. The museum contains old steam engines, restaurant cars, veteran cars and bicycles.

Hermanus (F3), much loved seaside resort with old fishing port (historical monument). Good opportunities for aquatic sports and surf-fishing. Abundant flora.

Hluhluwe Game Reserve (C9), in northern Zululand, particularly rich in white and black rhinoceroses.

Hopetown (D5), is famous as the place where South Africa's first diamond was discovered in 1866. The Pioneers' Cemetery 9 miles outside the town is a reminder of the diamond-rush.

Hout Bay (F3), bay on west coast of the Peninsula and holiday resort with beautiful beaches and harbour for lobster fishermen.

Howick Falls (D8), near Pietermaritzburg. The Umgeni River plunges over a 95 m (310 ft) cliff. Situated

near road. Observation platform, caravan park.

Inanda (D8), 12 miles north of Durban, the Mahatma Gandhi Museum commemorating the actions of the 21-year old Ghandi (1893–1914) on behalf of the Indian plantation workers.

Jeffreys Bay (F7), beach near Port Elizabeth famous for surfing and mussels.

Johannesburg (B7), largest city in South Africa with 2 million inhabitants. Financial and commercial centre of the country, largest industrial centre in the whole of Africa. Johannesburg owes its founding in 1886 to the goldfield – the largest on earth – that lies beneath its streets and in the immediate vicinity. The city is characterized by the yellow slagheaps and the pit-heads. The city, replete with American-style office and administration high-risers, has been laid out like a chess-board. In the suburbs are Bantu townships, like Soweto, where more than one million "natives" live. Main business quarter around Commissioner and Eloff streets and the Carlton Centre

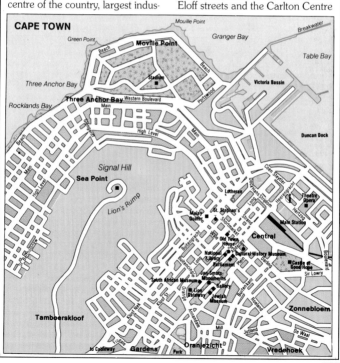

CAPE TOWN

129

which presents a good view of the city from the observation platform on its 49th floor. Several interesting museums are located in the Public Library in Market street: the Africana, the Archaeological and the Geological museums, the latter with a collection of gold samples and the Draper Precious Stone Collection. The Transport Museum in Pioneers Park has an exhibition with specimens from ox-wagons to steam engines. Railway Museum in Central Station. Art Gallery in Joubert Park. Two universities. A special attraction that is typical of the "gold town": a Gold Mining Museum, gold-mine and mining village all in one. On Sundays the traditional Dance of the Miners takes place there.

Kalahari Gemsbok National Park (B3/4), second largest game reserve in South Africa, located in the semi-desert of the Kalahari on with border with Botswana.

Karoo, the Hottentot word for dry and desolate, describes the vast dry steppe country that descends terrace-like from the Orange River down to the Cape. Initially as the **Upper Karoo** as far as the Great Escarpment at Roggeveld, Nuweveld and Sneuberg mountains (E4,5). Then as the **Great Karoo** up to the Swartberg mountains (f4) and finally as the **Little Karoo** between the Swartberg and the Langeberg mountain ranges (F4,5).

Karoo National Park (E4), conservation area near Beaufort West for the unique plantlife of the Great Karoo. Set up in 1979 and covering 70 square miles. About 50 species of game including mountain zebras, gemsboks, springboks and many small mammals.

+ **Keetmanshoop** (C3), fourth largest town in Namibia and important junction. Founded by the Germans in 1860, it became a garrison in 1884. Still many well-maintained buildings from the German colonial era. Centre of the foremost caracul breeding region in Namibia.

+ **Khorixas,** capital of Damaraland in the north of Namibia. Modern holiday camp. Good starting point for excursions to the Petrified Forest and the prehistoric paintings at Twyfelfontein (cf same).

Kimberley (D6), the "diamond city" with the Big Hole: 800 m (2,600 ft) deep – water up to 650 m (2,100 ft) – and 500 m (1,600 ft) across, it is the biggest hole ever created by human hand. From 1871 till 1915 about 3 tons of diamonds were extracted from it. Today it forms part of an interesting open air museum with displays from the days of the diamond-rush.

Knysna (F5), small port along the Garden Route. Centre of the stinkwood and yellowwood-working industry, as well as of a holiday area with ample forest and lakes. Lagoon, ideal for aquatic sports.

+ **Kokerboom Forest** (B3), about 14 miles north-east of Keetmanshoop. Some 300 specimens of this rare and strange tree – aloe dichotoma – can be seen in the grounds of Gariganus Farm. This copse – some of the trees are 8 m (26 ft) tall – is an historical monument.

+ **Kolmanskop** (C1), "ghost town" a few miles south-east of Lüderitz Bay next to a diamond-mine. Following the closing down of the mine the inhabitants moved away and the dunes moved in, but still well preserved.

Kruger National Park (A/B/8/9), South Africa's largest game reserve, both in size and in variety of game, situated in the Low Veld of eastern Transvaal on the border to Mozambique (cf p. 96).

Krugersdorp (B7), Town in gold mining region of Witwatersrand. Game reserve. Nearby are the geologically and archaeologically significant Sterkfontein stalactite caves.

Kyalami (B7), race track between Johannesburg and Pretoria that is scene of one of the Grand Prix races for formula one cars.

Lambert's Bay (E3), Fishing port on west coast with an island on which thousands of penguins and cormorants live.

Langebaan (F3 and map on p. 128), small village which gives its name to the 10 mile long Langebaan Lagoon which is a haven for many kinds of birds including European migratory birds and flamingoes.

Loskop Dam Nature Reserve (B7), leisure centre, game and nature reserve with rhinos and giraffes. Accommodation in bungalows. Caravan park, swimming, fishing and tennis.

+ **Lüderitz Bay** (C1), natural harbour on edge of Namib Desert. Once the centre of fishing and diamond mining industries, the place has lost considerably in importance. Popular holiday resort with good opportunities for bird-watching. Colony of seals.

Lydenburg (B8), "Town of snorrows" in memory of the difficult period of its founding in 1849. Lies shielded in a fertile valley and is famous for its trout fishing.

Margate (E8), like its English counterpart a popular seaside resort. Located on the "hibiscus coast" between Port Edward and Port Shepstone in the southern half of Natal.

Matjiesfontein (F4), health resort and Victorian village in the Karoo with many old loving-maintained buildings.

Messina (A8), South Africa's most northerly town on the frontier with Zimbabwe. Centre of the cooper mining industry and renowned for several baobab trees – more commonly called monkey-bread trees – in the vicinity that are up to 19 m (62 ft) in circumference and 26 m (85 ft) in height.

Mkuzi Game Reserve (C9), in north Zululand offers observation posts for watching the animals. Hikes through the wilderness (see map on p. 96).

Montagu (F3), holiday resort with radio active springs. Western gateway to the Little Karoo. Centre of fruit and wine country. Montagu Museum showing beautiful old furniture. Cape Dutch houses.

Mossel Bay (F4), port and popular resort at the western-most point of the Garden Route. Famous on several accounts: as Bartholomaus Diaz' landing place in 1488, for the Post Office Tree – sailors' letters used to be placed in boots that hung from the tree –, for its mussels and Mussel Museum with hundreds of specimens. Seal island.

Mountain Zebra National Park (E6), although established in 1937 to protect the mountain zebra other game is present in large numbers, especially antelopes and wildcats.

Muizenberg (F3), long white-sand beaches make it one of the most popular resorts on False Bay.

+ **Mukorob** (B2), "Finger of God" in the Nama tongue, a strange weather-formed stone pillar 34 m (110 ft) high, one of most remarkable landmarks in south Namibia.

Naboomspruit (B7), Trans-Orange bird sanctuary with many indigenous and exotic species.

+ **Namib-Naukluft Park** (A/B/1/2) created in 1978 when the Namib Desert Park was linked up to the Naukluft Mountain Zebra Park. Stretches eastwards from Swakopmund and Walvis Bay into the Naukluft mountains. One of the most unusual nature and game reserves with the highest dunes in the Namib Desert (cf p. 96)

Ndedema Gorge (D7), high valley in Natal's Drakenberg mountains near Cathedral Peak with 17 rock faces and caves containing 4,000 rock paintings showing the prehistoric art of the Bushmen.

Ndumu Game Reserve (C9), Zululand's most northerly reserve on the border to Mozambique. Particularly rich birdlife. (cf p. 96).

Nelspruit (B8), commercial centre in eastern Transvaal and point of departure for visiting the Kruger National Park. Located in Crocodile River valley where the subtropical climate favours citrus fruits, tobacco, mangoes, papayas, etc. Botanical garden with flowers from the Low Veld.

Oribi Gorge Nature Reserve (E8), one of Natal's best scenic attractions: a 16 mile long, 3 mile wide and in places 500 m (1,650 ft) deep gorge cut into the Oribi plateau by the Umzimkulu River. The upper ridge presents many magnificent views of the green valley and its animals – principally antelopes including the oribi that once lived here in great numbers. Rest camp.

Oudtshoorn (F4), important town in the Little Karoo and the only place in the world where ostriches are bred successfully. Several farms offer an insight into the "ostrich industry" (cf p. 140).

Paarl (F3), centre of one of the most important wine-growing regions in South Africa and scene of many large vaults, including the biggest in the world, K.W.V. Many beautiful Cape Dutch houses set in orchards and vineyards, not to mention those in the centre of the town, like "Oude Pastorie", now a museum, and "strooidakkerk" – literally, straw roof church. Drakenstein mountains and the granite pinnacle, Britannia Rock.

Papatso (B7), native village 30 miles north of Pretoria. Handicrafts centre with good opportunities for shopping.

+ **Petrified Forest,** petrified weather-beaten tree-trunks estimated to be 200 million years old situated west of Khorixas in Namibia. The rare welwitschia grows here too.

Pietermaritzburg (D8), capital of Natal founded in 1838. The red brick City Hall is both an historical monument and the city's emblem. Other historically interesting buildings include the Voortrekker Museum in the "Church of the Vow" and the Victorian style Macrorie House Museum (1861–63) showing furniture and tools of the early British settlers. Botanical garden.

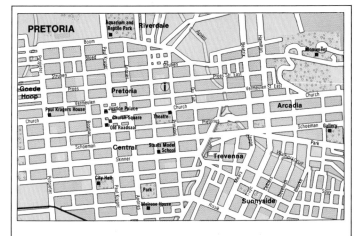

Pilgrim's Rest (B8), historic village in Transvaal's Drakenberg mountains that recalls the days of the gold-rush in 1874. The main street and the Betha Mine have been carefully restored.

Plettenberg Bay (F5), on the Garden Route west of Port Elizabeth. Has three long beaches and is one of the country's favourite holiday resorts.

Port Elizabeth (F6), largest city in eastern part of Cape Province, third largest port in South Africa and the most easterly point along the Garden route. Very English with early settler's houses, the oldest of which is no. 7, Castle Hill built in 1872. Victorian houses in Donkin Street. The city's emblem is the 52 m (170 ft) high bell-tower commemorating colonization in 1820. Extensive multilane city motorway. Modern skyline. Beautiful beaches and amusement arcades.

Pretoria (B7), seat of South African government, capital of the Province of Transvaal. With 750,000 inhabitants the fourth largest city in the country. University. Centre of research, scholarship and art. Historical mementos of the famous Boer president, Paul "Oom" Kruger: his residence in Church Street is furnished with innumerable pieces of his fittings and effects: Paul Kruger Memorial in Church Square. Splendid furniture from the Victorian-Edwardian period can be viewed in Melrose House, an early stately house constructed in 1883. The Union Buildings on Meintjeskop are amongst the loveliest of their kind. Transvaal Museum with voluminous natural history, geological and archaeological collections, as well as a valuable exhibition of precious stones. The many parks and most of the streets are full of jacaranda-trees, and Pretoria is covered with a soft blue and lilac veil during blossom-time in October and November. South of the city stands the Voortrekker Memorial as a reminder of the Great Trek.

Prieska (D5), small town on the banks of the river Orange that enjoys a world-wide reputation for high quality semi-precious stones, above all tiger's-eye, found in the area.

Prince Albert (F4), pretty, old town at the foot of the Swartberg mountains with many Cape Dutch buildings and an old watermill.

Randburg (B7), a suburb in northwest Johannesburg whose Kleinjukskei Vintage car Museum houses an interesting collection of veteran vehicles.

Robertson (F4), a holiday resort and wine-growing community that is beautifully located in the Breede River Valley and possesses the biggest distillery in South Africa.

Royal Natal National Park (D7), one of the most beautiful nature parks in the Drakensberg mountains, famous for the vast amphitheatre in the Mont-aux-Sources massif. Plenty of animals and plants, hiking trails. Bushman rock paintings.

Rust der Winter Nature Reserve (B7), reserve with great variety of birdlife.

Sabie (B8), charmingly situated little town on one of the terrasses of the Drakensberg mountains in Transvaal overlooked by the 2,285 m (7,490 ft) high Mount Anderson. Sabie owes its existence to a gold-mine that was abandoned in 1950 and its present popularity to the lovely surrounding countryside of widespread forests and waterfalls: Lone Creek

Falls, Bridal Veil Falls and the Mac-Mac Falls (see map on p. 140).

Sodwana Bay National Park (C9), small somewhat remote reserve in north-eastern Natal that deserves a visit because of its birdlife.

Springbok (D2), principal city of Namaqualand. Encircled by granite mountains. Centre of copper mining industry (historic smelting furnace dating from 1866). The spring blossom – August or September depending on the rain – is spectacular, especially the many species and colours of daisies.

Stellenbosch (F3), second oldest city in the country and one of the most beautiful historic places with many Cape Dutch buildings and old oaks. Central point is the town square – or "Braak" – around which are grouped such historic buildings as the Burger House, Powder Magazine, the Anglican church of St. Mary's, Rhenish Church and Coachman's cottage. Stellenbosch Museum in Grosvenor House. Wine Museum in Dorp Street which also contains two further examples of classical Cape Dutch architecture: Libertas Parva (with a gallery from the Rembrandt van Rijn Foundation) and La Gratitude. Important university. Stellenbosch is the centre of a wine region with many vineyards and the starting point of the wine route of the same name.

St. Lucia Game Reserve (C/D9), in an estuary in Zululand. Hippos, crocodiles and various species of waterfowl and birds of prey (cf p. 96).

Strijdom Tunnel (B8), named after Prime Minister J. G. Strijdom. It forms part of the Abel Erasmus Pass that crosses the Drakensberg and overcomes a drop in altitude of 800 m (2,600 ft) while descending into the Low Veld.

Sudwala Caves (B8), famous for the strangely shaped stalactites such as "The Screaming Ghost" and "The Weeping Lady". The P. R. Owen Chamber is large enough – 18 m (60 ft) high, 66 m (215 ft) diameter – for concerts to be held in it.

+ **Swakopmund** (A1), once the chief port of South West Africa and now Namibia's most popular seaside resort offering a refreshing refuge from the heat of the interior. The city is still very German in character, as witnessed by such relics as the lighthouse (the city's emblem), the Evangelist Church, the railway station built in 1901, the Woermann House (nowadays a library) as well as a great number of old half-timbered houses with hip-roofs. The museum contains interesting collections showing the history of Swakopmund and Namibia, besides specimens of the fauna and flora of the Namib Desert and the sea.

Swellendam (F4), historically and architecturally intriguing town. Drostdy, built as the seat of the new magistracy in 1747, now a museum with over 2,000 exhibition pieces depicting the history of Swellendam as the third oldest city in South Africa after Cape Town and Stellenbosch. The Bontebok National Park is nearby (cf p. 140).

Tulbagh (F3), principal township in a pretty viniculture valley flanked by the Witsenberg, Winterhoekberg and the Saronsberg mountain ranges. Founded in 1699 the town was almost completely destroyed by one of South Africa's rare earthquakes

in 1969. It was re-built to its former beauty and today the 32 restored houses in Kerk Street make it one of the best maintained old streets in Cape Province.

Tsitsikamma Coastal National Park (F5), the first of its kind in Africa, encompasses the coast of southern Cape Province for 50 miles running parallel to the Garden Route from Plettenberg Bay to Humansdorp. The 800 m (880 yd) wide strip of coastline embraces cliffs, ravines, brooks and ponds. The animals and flowers protected within its boundaries include otters, badgers, small antelopes and various monkeys; heather, proteas, orchids, lilies, ferns and gigantic yellowwood-trees.

Tsitsikamma Forest National Park (F5), is not far from the coastal park and was established to protect one of the last jungles comprising mighty old yellowwood and stinkwood trees ("Big Tree"), shrubs, creepers and lichen. Several short hiking trails.

Tsonga Kral (A8), a museum in the Hans Merensky Nature Reserve consisting of typical native huts that are properly furnished and in which the dwellers exercise traditional handicrafts like pottery and basketry.

+ **Twyfelfontein,** site of significant rock art paintings and engravings in the north-west of Namibia. Thousands of drawings of giraffes, rhinos, springboks, etc, scratched into the rock face about 1,000 to 5,000 years ago are attributed to the Hottentots.

Uitenhage (F6), founded in 1804, possesses a lovely Cape Dutch drostdy (residence and offices of the Landdrost – a district commissioner) that is now used as a museum containing a valuable bible printed in 1819. The park on Cannon Hill displays a great number of South African cactuses. The old railway station houses a Train Museum.

Umfolozi Game Reserve (D9), in northern Zululand, is a conservation area principally for white and black rhinoceroses. Hikes through the wilderness. (cf p. 96).

Upington (C4), agricultural centre on the river Orange in north-west Cape Province. Stepping off point for trips to the Kalahari Gemsbok National Park (cf p. 140) and the Augrabie Falls National Park.

Valley of a Thousand Hills (D8), well known for its beautiful scenery. A vast expanse of lowland with countless rolling hills interspersed with native villages. Organised tours from Durban come here to see the Zulu dances.

Valley of Desolation (E5), one of the most remarkable examples of natural erosion in South Africa. Rugged cliffs and bizarre basalt pillars overlooked by the uniquely shaped Spandau Head. Historical monument on the edge of the Karoo near Graaf Reinet. The Karoo Nature Reserve is part of the valley.

+ **Vingerklip** ("Finger Rock"), 35 m (115 ft) high eroded finger-shaped stone formation in northern Namibia about 60 miles west of Outjo.

Walvis Bay (A1), an enclave of the Republic on the west coast of Namibia. As a deep sea port it is Namibia's most important access to the sea. Fishing centre. Lagoon with many kinds of waterfowl, including flamingoes and pelicans.

+ **Waterberg Plateau Park**, a

long mountain ridge with such rare wild animals as the white rhinoceros, roan and sable antelopes. Rock paintings and engravings.

Welkom (C6), gold-mining centre in Orange Free State. Wealth of birdlife around the gold-mine dams.

White, groaning sands (D4), white dunes 8 miles long and 2 miles wide

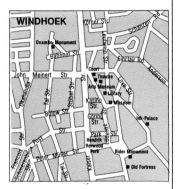

in the middle of the red sand dunes of the Kalahari (strangely the two types of sand do not mix). If you touch or move the sand, for example with your hand or by walking on it, a groaning, grunting noise is emitted – albeit only in summer.

Wilderness (F4/5), one of the most popular holiday resorts along the Garden Route. The wide 5 mile long beach is more suited to walking than bathing on account of the under-currents. Forests and lakes as far as Knysna.

Willem Pretorius Game Reserve (C6/7), at the Allemanskraal Dam in eastern Orange Free State (cf p. 96).

+ **Windhoek** (A2), the capital of

136

Namibia with almost 90,000 inhabitants lies at an altitude of 1,700 m (5,600 ft) sheltered by the Auas and Eros mountain ranges. Modern western town with obvious and architecturally charming reminders of the German colonial era (1884–1915); names like Kaiser Street (the main road), Christus Church, Alte Feste (once a fort, now a museum), the Tintenpalast (literally, Palace of Ink that is still used for administration), the Reiter Memorial, cosy beergardens and a number of lovely old houses with verandas. Moreover, the women of the Herero tribe still wear the colourful Victorian style of dress introduced by the missionaries.

Worcester (F3), largest community in the Breede River Valley. Important centre for fruit and wine. A little outside the town is the Botanical Garden of the Karoo where wild flowers and plants from the arid areas of South Africa can be seen. One of the five internationally recognized gardens for succulents in the world.

Social Customs

Every country in the world has its own unwritten laws and visitors should know and respect them, if they do not wish to appear boorish.

South African women are fairly reserved in public and in traditional male spheres:

– for example, ladies do not go into bars either alone or even accompanied by men. For them and their companions there are **Ladies Lounges.** It is always the man who does the inviting.

– Ladies are not seen in public in **excessively scanty clothing,** not even on the beach. Topless bathing is officially forbidden.

– Men should remember that it is not always correct to appear in casual clothes, ie **without jacket and tie** – no matter how hot it may be. Obviously, this does not apply on safaris or in the game lodges.

– **correct dress** is expected at meal times in good **restaurants** and private clubs – especially during the evenings.

– It is not usual in South Africa to look for a **seat in a restaurant.** One should wait until a member of the staff shows one to a table – even if this demands a little more time.

– it is usual to give a **tip** in hotels and restaurants, unless 10% has been included in the bill. The amount is up to you and depends on the service. Native chambermaids and other native hotel staff take their tips with both hands open – a traditional gesture of thanks.

– You should only **photograph people** – and this applies particularly to non-whites – if you feel that they will not mind or at least will not be bothered. If you are not sure, then ask politely. If there are language problems, your guide or, if you are alone, sign language will help.

Pornogaphy and the exhibiting of naked bodies in any form is forbidden in South Africa. Even if you hold other views, please respect theirs.

(TAR)

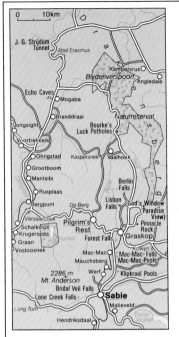

Reading list

Information/Illustration guides:
Reader's Digest – Reader's Digest illustrated Guide to Southern Africa
Dennis Conolly – Conolly's Guide to Southern Africa
Pocket guides:
Berlitz – Travel Guide South Africa
Thomas E. King – South Africa in your Pocket
Colour picture books:
Gerald and Arnold Helfet – South Africa
Jean Morris – South Africa
Jean Morris – Scenic South Africa
CNA/Struik – Panoramic South Africa
Reader's Digest – Southern Africa, Land of Beauty and Splendour
August Sycholt, Peter Schirmer – This is South Africa

South Africa

The following denominations are currently in use:
Notes: Rand 2, 5, 10, 20, 50
      (The 1 Rand note has been withdrawn from
      circulation.)
Coins: Cent 1, 2, 5, 10, 20, 50, Rand 1

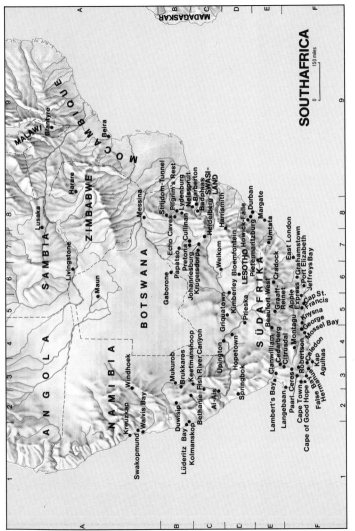

SOUTHAFRICA

0 ___ 150 miles

MADAGASKAR

MALAWI
Blantyre

MOÇAMBIQUE
Beira

ZAMBIA
Lusaka
Livingstone

ZIMBABWE
Harare

Maun

ANGOLA

NAMIBIA
Windhoek
Kreuzkap
Swakopmund
Walvis Bay
Lüderitz Bay
Kolmanskop
Duwisib
Bethanie
Al-Ais
Fish River-Canyon
Keetmanshoop
Brukkaros
Mukurob

BOTSWANA
Gaborone
Messina

Springbok
Upington
Hopetown
Griquatown

Echo Caves
Strijdom-Tunnel
Pilgrim's Rest
Lydenburg
Nelspruit
Barberton
Badplaas
SWASI-
LAND
Papatso
Pretoria
Cullinan
Johannesburg
Krugersdorp
Heidelberg
Harrismith

Welkom
Kimberley
Bloemfontein
LESOTHO
Howick-Fälle
Pietermaritzburg
Pieska
Durban
Margate

SÜDAFRIKA
Beaufort West
Cradock
Umtata
Graaff-
Reinet
East London
Clanwilliam
Cedarberg
Citrusdal
Montagu
Robertson
Apple
Express
Grahamstown
Port Elizabeth
Jeffreys Bay
Knysna
Cap St.
Francis
George
Mossel Bay

Lambert's Bay
Langebaan
Paarl
Ceres
Cape Town
Cape of Good Hope
False Bay
Caledon
Hermanus
Kap
Agulhas

140

Useful Information

Currency

1 Rand(R) = 100 cents
£1 = R1.80
US$ = ca. R1.35

Pound sterling and US$ rates are indicated, in order to give you a general idea as to the value of the local currency. However, you should, before setting off on your holiday, find out from your own bankers what the present rate of exchange, your currency to Rand, is.

Exchange Control Regulations

South African money can be imported and exported up to R200. Foreign currency is unlimited, although the amount taken out may not exceed that brought in. Changing money does not usually present any problem in banks or hotels. It is advisable to take all the money you will need in the form of Travellers Cheques. If these are in Rand, they will not be counted as local currency on entry.

Travellers Cheques, Bankers Cards

Travellers Cheques in US$ or any other western currency will be accepted by all banks, good hotels, restaurants and shops. However, cheques, even if supported by a banker's card, are not acceptable.

Credit Cards

The use of credit cards is widespread, especially in restaurants, hotels and shops frequented by foreign customers. Almost all cards are accepted, but Visa, Diners Club and Mastercard probably offer the widest network.

Passport and Visas

All visitors require a valid passport, and most will need a visa as well. One exeption: holders of United Kingdom passports who are of Caucasian, ie white descent. Contact the South African Embassy or one of the consulates when planning your trip.

Visitors are issued with a temporary residence permit valid for 90 days on arrival.

Visiting South Africa's Neighbours

With the possible exception of South West Africa (Namibia), South Africa's neighbouring countries are normally reached from the Republic itself. Most of these countries (Botswana, Lesotho, Swaziland, Bophuthatswana, Ciskei, Venda and the Transkei) do not have customs controls, but the situation regarding entry is less clear and in cases of doubt, you are advised to contact your diplomatic post in South Africa.

A look at the principal countries individually:

Bophuthatswana. Visas do not appear to be necessary for most visitors at the time of writing. Should the regulations have altered, a visa can be quickly and easily obtained at the Bophuthatswana Embassy, 39 Glyn Street, Colbyn, Pretoria 0001; Tel: 43–60 01 or from the Consulate-General, North City Building, corner Plein and Klein streets, Johannesburg 2001; Tel: 23–17 67. Should you be flying in to Sun City, visas are also issued at the Jan Smuts International Airport at Johannesburg. For those arriving by car the official check point, Willow Park, is only open from 6 am to 8 pm, though there are hundreds of other crossing points into the six different parts of Bophuthatswana – mostly without control posts.

Botswana, Lesotho, Swaziland and Namibia all demand only a valid passport. Incidentally, anyone wishing to visit Namibia can use the regular shuttles from Johannesburg and Cape Town to Windhoek's J. G. Strydom airport.

Visitors to Botswana, Lesotho and Swaziland will, however, require an International Certificate of Vaccination for smallpox.

In addition to the service provided by SAA to Maseru from Johannesburg on Monday, Wednesday and Friday and to Manzini from Durban on Friday, Swazi Air also operate daily services between Johannesburg and Manzini and between Durban and Manzini on Mondays.

Except for Sunday there are daily flights between Johannesburg and Gaborone in Botswana.

Those intending to tour the northern part of Namibia should obtain anti-malarial tablets from local chemists and start taking them a few days before going into this area.

Transkei. The authorities probably require visitors to have visas and to enter at specified places. These visas can be obtained at the Transkei Consulate-General, Kariba House, Johannesburg 2001; Tel: 21–59 35 or at the Consulates in Durban, Port Elizabeth, Bloemfontein, Cape Town and East London. If you are travelling through the Transkei on The N2 you can also get a visa at the check point.

The situation for entering **Ciskei, Venda** and the other independent Homelands is uncertain and you are again advised to contact your Embassy or one of the Consulates-General.

General Caution. Travellers whose passports show that they have visited South Africa – or intend to do so – may well be refused entry into Algeria, Angola, Cameroon, Guinea, Nigeria, Sudan, Tanzania and other African countries. Should this be likely to cause difficulties on this or future journeys,

you should seek advice at your passport offices.

As entry regulations are liable to change at short notice, it is advisable to get the latest information from your local travel agent or the diplomatic offices of the country or countries you wish to include on your itinerary before leaving.

Health control
Vaccination is not necessary unless travelling from one of the yellow fever zones. If entering Swaziland from South Africa you may be asked to present proof of vaccination against cholera. It is advisable to take precautions against malaria, if travelling to the Low Veld in Transvaal (Kruger Park) or Natal (Zululand). The doctor carrying out the vaccination will advise you about the best anti-malarial medicines and their reaction to particularly resient types of the sickness.

When making your holiday arrangements, don't forget to ask the travel agent about public health regulations currently in force in the country/countries you wish to visit or will transit. If he isn't quite sure, then call either the embassy, consulate or government sponsored tourist office of the country/ies you'll be visiting, and ask. They'll be pleased to assist you; and forewarned is forearmed.

In case of illness
Medical care is very good, but there is no bi-lateral agreement on social services with South Africa. If treatment is necessary, go as a private patient and ask for a receipt.

It is a good idea to take out Travel Sickness Insurance, possibly combined with an Accident and Luggage Insurance. Your local travel agency or insurance agent will be glad to give you further information.

Language

The official languages of South Africa are English and Afrikaans, but you will rarely meet anyone who does not speak English. German is still widely used and understood in Namibia. The most spoken African languages are Zulu and Xhosa.

Car rentals

In addition to the information given in the chapter entitled: "Travel in South Africa – a Pleasure" here are some prices as at August 1983. A Metro or Vauxhall Astra cost approx. R13 a day. A Jaguar XJ12 with air-conditioning approx. R75 a day. If you book your car before leaving, the price for one week including unlimited mileage, Third Party Liability insurance and Full Cover with self-participation of R300 will work out between £100/US$130 and £250/US$330. A mobile home (Autovilla) with 120 free miles daily costs about £200/US$260 a week. The minimum age for renting cars is 23. Although most foreign driving licences are recognized, it is advisable to obtain an International Driving Licence through a motoring organization. Petrol is available all over South Africa and garages are open from 7 am to 6 pm. Outside these hours some petrol stations will fill your tank for an extra R5.00

Taxis

The initial charge varies from town to town and is between 60 and 90 cents, plus 60 to 90 cents per kilometre. Taxis do not cruise round looking for custom, but must be ordered from the taxi stands.

Business hours

Banks in the cities 9 am to 3.30 pm Monday through Friday (Wednesday till 1 pm), and 8.30 am to 11 am on Saturday. In the country 9 am to 12.45 am on Monday, Tuesday, Thursday and Friday. Wednesday and Saturday as in the city.

Post offices Mon–Fri 8.30 am–1 pm and 2 pm–4.30 pm. Sat 8 am–12 am. In the cities some post offices remain open at lunch-time.

Shops Mon–Fri 8.30 am–5 pm, Sat 8.30 am–12.45 am or 1 pm. Greengrocers, book shops, chemists and some supermarkets have longer opening hours. Coffee shops from 6 am to midnight (Sundays to 9 pm).

Service charges and tipping

Most restaurants usually include a 10% service charge in the bill. If they hold a liquor licence, they are prevented by law from including a service charge for any alcohol consumed.

If the restaurant bill does include a service charge (if in doubt, ask), the amount is generously rounded up. If the service was very good, this can be as much as 10%. Should the service not be included in the bill, it is normal to add 10%–15%. Taxi-drivers also get 10%. Generally speaking, there is less tipping than in Europe or the USA, though this is gradually changing. Luggage porters and chambermaids are pleased to receive 50 cents or R1 per piece of luggage or day respectively and often show their gratitude by placing their open hands, palm upwards, together.

Postal charges

Airmail post cards cost 15 cents. Airmail letters 20 cents for every 10 grams.

Telegrams cost 24 cents a word.

Telephone. With the exception of remote country areas, it is possible to dial direct to practically any country in the world from most places in South Africa.

Electricity supply

Mainly 220/230 volts, AC 50 cycles, but in Pretoria 250 volts and in Port

Elizabeth 220/250 volts. In some areas, for example rest camps in various national parks and game reserves, adapters are required.

Clothing

Clothing should be suitable for a warm mild climate – lightweight tropical suits during the day, and cardigans, light pullovers, wraps and medium-weight suits during cool evenings, especially at high altitudes in the winter months or in air-conditioned rooms. Casual clothing is best for guided tours, holiday resorts and game reserves. More formal clothing is preferable in town during the evening as well as in some restaurants and hotels in the resorts. Men are expected to wear a jacket and tie at all mealtimes and after 6 pm. (Even if you object to wearing a tie on holiday, take one with you to be on the safe side!). Women should not appear too scantily dressed in public – not even on the beach. And, by the way, "topless" ist prohibited by law.

School holidays in South Africa

South Africans love travelling and take advantage of the school holidays to move around with the family. This can lead to bottle-necks for accommodation in the major holiday areas such as the coast of Natal or the Kruger National Park, making it necessary to book well in advance. The biggest holiday crowds occur when the schools in the Transvaal (the cities of Johannesburg and Pretoria) break up.

Christmas Holidays: beginning December till mid-January.

Easter Holidays: approx. 3 weeks around Easter.

Winter Holidays: whole of July, possibly up to early August.

The holidays of the other three provinces are one week later at the most and are made up by "September Holidays" lasting a week (between September/October). Exact dates can be obtained from SATOUR.

Taking photographs

All the well-known international makes of film are available. It is usually possible to have your films developed right away. In any event should take all the film you need with you. If you intend using a tele-objective (180 mm and over) to photograph animals, don't forget to take a High Sensitivity film – 200 or 400 ASA. To reduce blurring and get background sharpness, choose a short exposure time and a small aperture. The same procedure should be adhered to for close-ups of flowers, small animals, etc. It does not normally cause problems to photograph people, if you approach them openly and amicably and don't "ambush" them. A few words, a smile or even a look will tell you whether they mind being photographed or not. Should they object, accept and respect their point of view. Tribal dances can best be photographed in the Gold Mine Museum in Johannesburg (Sundays only) or at Stewart's Farm during the course of an excursion from Durban.

Customs Regulations

Into South Africa. In addition to your personal belongings you may import the following free of duty:

– new or used merchandise up to a total value of R80 as well as 1 litre of alcohol, including liqueurs and hard drinks

– 1 litre of wine in opened or unopened bottles

– 400 cigarettes or 50 cigars or 250 grams (9 ozs) of tobacco

– 300 milli-litres of parfume.

What you may take with you by way of duty-free articles and other goods on returning home from South Africa will depend on the local customs regulations.

Before departure it is a good idea to ask the customs staff for a detailed brochure containing up-to-date regulations.

Crime
South Africa has not been spared completely from a certain amount of crime in the cities, even though the incidence is low. For instance, in Johannesburg, the city with the biggest percentage of "natives", crime is mostly amongst the blacks but can also occur between blacks and whites. For this reason avoid lonely streets in the cities at night and take a taxi for short distances, even if you feel like "getting a breathe of fresh air". Above all, never make a show of valuables such as expensive watches, and only carry as much cash with you as is needed. Deposit your jewellery, cash, Travellers Cheques, etc in the hotel safe that is usually free of charge. You can leave your passport there as well, as long as you carry photocopies of the most important pages around with you.

Airport charges
Are not levied for international flights.

Important addresses
Any tourist information office, or your travel agent, will be able to let you know exactly where your embassy or consulate is located; it's very useful to have the address and telephone number to hand, in case of loss or damage to personal property or effects – or should you require repatriation!

Recommended Itineraries
Johannesburg. The journey begins in Johannesburg, largest city in the country. The following day an excursion to **Pretoria** – the governmental city.

Visit to a gold-mine on the **Witwatersrand** before flying on to **Kimberley.**

Visit to the famous **De Beers Diamond Mine** and the **"Big Hole".**

Visit to the **Duggan-Cronin-Bantu Gallery** (ethnographical museum). Fly to **Cape Town.** Tour South Africa's mother-city with drive up to **Table Mountain.** Go shopping or take a stroll in the afternoon.

Day trip to the **Cape of Good Hope.**

Plettenberg Bay. Fly to **Oudtshoorn.** Visit the **Cango Caves** and an **ostrich farm.**

Drive to Plettenberg Bay. Next day: rest and sun-bathe.

Drive to **Port Elizabeth** passing through the Storms **River Gorge** and the **Tsitsikamma Nature Reserve.** Fly to **Durban.** Sightseeing round the largest port (Indian market). Lunch in an Indian restaurant. Drive on to the **Valley of 1,000 Hills.** Visit the **Phezulu Kraal** showing the living habits of a Zulu tribe.

Two day rest on the beaches around Durban. (From here there is a choice of three itineraries.)

Hluhluwe. Start of a **safari** along the northern coast of **Natal** including Zulu dances in a **kraal,** hunting trip in the game reserves of **Mkuze, Hluhuwe** or **Umfolozi.**

Mbabane. Drive into the Kingdom of **Swaziland.** Opportunity to go to the **casino.**

Kruger National Park. Whole day **safari.** Spend the night in Rondavels.

Blyde River Canyon. Cross the **Kowyn Pass,** view the **Berlin** and **Lisbon waterfalls** and breath-taking scenes in the **canyon.**

Johannesburg. Return through the wooded mountain country via **Pilgrim's Rest.**

Alternative itinerary from Durban: 1 day stay in **Windhoek, Etosha Pan,** stay for several days in the biggest game reserve in the world.

Fly back to **Windhoek.**

Flight back home.

Alternatively, visit Zimbabwe after Durban. Sightseeing around **Harare** (Salisbury) with excursions to the **Larvon Bird Gardens,** the **Lion and Cheetah Park,** and to the **Lake McIllwaine Game Park.** Day trip in airplane to the **ruins** of the old Kingdom of Zimbabwe.

Hwange (Wankie). Fly to the Hwange (Wankie) National Park, observe and photograph animals.

Victoria Falls. Fly to the magnificent waterfalls, **boot trip** on the Zambesi in the afternoon, native **dancing.** Walk through the **rain forest** opposite the falls or take a **10 minute trip** over the falls in a sports plane.

Return flight home via **Johannesburg.**

Contents

Map

Attention!
All prices and currency indications were accurate at the time of printing.
As it is not possible for any travel guide to keep up with the constantly
changing rates of exchange, you are advised to contact your bank
regarding the current rates.
The publishers would be pleased to have your opinion regarding any
omissions or alterations.

Personal Notes

Personal Notes

Personal Notes

Personal Notes

Personal Notes

Personal Notes

Personal Notes

Personal Notes

Personal Notes